Looki for Githa

By Patricia Riley

New Writing North

new
writing
north

About the author

Pat Riley's love of theatre was instilled in her from an early age as both her parents were involved in the amateur theatre, and she has vivid memories of discovering the beauty of language by being taken regularly to the then Shakespeare Memorial Theatre from the age of eight. As an adult she obtained degrees in Law, Social Science and Management but retained her passion for theatre throughout her life. Now retired, she is Secretary of the Wharfedale Festival of Theatre and, with her husband, is an active member of an award-winning amateur dramatic society. She has three sons and seven grand-children.

First published in 2009 by
New Writing North
Holy Jesus Hospital
City Road
Newcastle upon Tyne
NE1 2AS
www.newwritingnorth.com

New Writing North Limited 3166037
Registered charity number 1062729

ISBN 978-0955882944

Editor: Rebecca Jenkins
Copy-editing and production design: John Adair

Printed in Great Britain by Cpod, Trowbridge, Wiltshire.
A division of The Cromwell Press Group.

Contents

Foreword by Richard Beecham

Preface

Foreword

By Richard Beecham

Director of the 2009 Tyneside revival of *Rutherford & Son*

Some years ago I was invited by my colleague Joanna Read to see her production of a play called *Rutherford & Son* at Salisbury Playhouse. Joanna knew that I was born and brought up in Newcastle upon Tyne and she thought I would like to see what she described as a forgotten Tyneside classic, a play I myself had never heard of, enjoying a rare revival. She was not wrong. Sitting at a weekday matinee amongst the somewhat genteel and elderly audience from this picturesque cathedral city in rural Wiltshire, I was astonished to encounter a ferocious Geordie drama thick with dialect, diatribe and an unsparing depiction of the brutalities of the industrial north at the turn of the century. I was riveted and not a little surprised.

Returning home I set about a bit of investigative work. What was known about the playwright, Githa Sowerby? Very little, it appeared, from my trawls through the British Library archives and the internet; there was no biography or critical work to be had. As far as the play's production history was concerned, it appeared that there had been only a handful of productions since its rediscovery in 1980 by a small feminist theatre company but, astonishingly, the play had never been performed on its native Tyneside. From a glance at the cast lists from previous productions it also became clear that this seminal Geordie drama had never been performed by native North East actors. It is widely recognised that the Geordie accent is the hardest of all the accents of the British Isles for actors to master with any degree of accuracy, and I felt immediately aggrieved that the proper music of Sowerby's play had never been heard by its audiences. Something needed to be done.

Nearly a decade after my first encounter with the play something is indeed being done, as *Rutherford & Son* returns home to Tyneside in a production by Northern Stage and Threshold Theatre. Almost a century after the 35-year-old Githa Sowerby sat down to pen her first play in 1911, *Rutherford & Son* will finally receive its North East premiere in 2009 in a production performed by a company of North East actors (no more cod Geordie accents mangling the text!). To mark this moment of cultural homecoming, a number of events have been planned to celebrate this unjustly neglected playwright and reinstate her into the canon of great Tyneside writers. Foremost of these is the publication of *Looking for Githa*, the first ever biography of the remarkable Githa Sowerby. Its author, Pat Riley, has done a truly splendid job in unearthing this compelling, and meticulously researched, account of

Githa's life and works. As the director of this revival of *Rutherford & Son*, I am indebted to her for the new light her research has shed on this great playwright and play. When I first began looking for Githa a decade ago I drew a frustrated blank, but this book will surely become the standard text for all future producers, students and scholars of Githa Sowerby's work.

Richard Beecham
Artistic Director
Threshold Theatre
July 2009

Preface

"Moloch was a sort of a god… They built his image with an ugly head ten times the size of a real head, with great wheels instead of legs, and set him up in the middle of a great dirty town. And they thought him a very important person indeed and made sacrifices to him - human sacrifices - to keep him going, you know. Out of every family they set aside one child to be an offering to him when it was big enough and at last it became a sort of honour to be dedicated in this way, so much so that the victims gave themselves gladly to be crushed out of life under the great wheels. That was Moloch."[1]

Rutherford & Son, Act 1

It was September 2007 when I first read in Act One of Githa Sowerby's most famous play, *Rutherford & Son,* that extraordinary denunciation of the legacy of the industrial revolution. I was immediately intrigued. *Rutherford & Son* had been a smash hit in the West End in 1912 at a time when women were widely believed to have been created solely for the procreation of children and the sexual satisfaction of men. What sort of Edwardian woman, as early as 1912, had dared to write with such savagery about domestic tyranny and the unacceptable face of capitalism?

In fact, how on earth had *Rutherford & Son* come to be produced at all? The theatre of 1912 was dominated by men who were accustomed to presenting plays that showed life exclusively from a male perspective, and they found being forced to look at the world as it appeared to women an unsettling and uncomfortable experience. Some feminist commentators[2] argue that it was these male responses, based on gender prejudice, that led to the systematic suppression of women's writing in the past through techniques such as doubting the possibility of female authorship, attacking the subject matter, or denying its right to be called art. This resonates with Githa's experience in that after her initial success with *Rutherford & Son,* her work was largely forgotten. It is only since the last two decades of the 20th century (and thanks in no small measure to the work of modern-day female directors including Katie Mitchell in England and Jackie Maxwell in Canada) that the theatrical and social significance of *Rutherford & Son* has been acknowledged. And even now, despite the growing recognition of her work, none of Githa's other full-length plays have ever been published in England.[i]

---

i Githa's 1924 play, *The Stepmother,* was published in Canada in 2008 by the Shaw Festival Theatre, Ontario.

Who was Githa Sowerby? I had to find out. The writing of *Rutherford &
Son* showed not only unusual political awareness and immense personal
courage, but quite a detailed knowledge of the technicalities of the glassmaking industry. How had Githa acquired such knowledge in an era when
keeping women in ignorant, fashionable idleness was a mark of social status?
A fortnight of fruitless searching for information about Githa Sowerby
soon told me that it was not just me who had no answers to those questions.
Nobody had.

The brief introduction to the script published by Methuen to coincide with the
National Theatre's 1994 production of *Rutherford & Son* informed the reader:

"Little is known about Githa Sowerby other than that she spent her
childhood in Tyne and Wear and her family were involved in the glassmaking business. It seems she moved to London in her early twenties and
probably wrote *Rutherford & Son* (1912) in her new southern location. Other
plays followed: *Before Breakfast* (1912), *A Man and Some Women* (1914), *Sheila*
(1917), *The Stepmother* (1924), *The Policeman's Whistle* (1934). From then on
she wrote numerous books for children with her elder sister Millicent. Githa
Sowerby died in 1970."

The introduction to this edition of the script also stated that *Rutherford &
Son* was set "in North Yorkshire". That couldn't possibly be right. It ignored
the Geordie dialect in which much of the play is written and a specific
reference in the dialogue to the River Tyne.

Instead of the enlightenment I sought, further research revealed that a web
of mystery and misinformation surrounded this early 20th century feminist
playwright and children's author. It also became clear that this state of affairs
had partly arisen because of the smokescreen put up by Githa herself to
protect her privacy. A book about illustrators of nursery postcards confidently
stated that Githa's sister Millicent (who was younger than Githa, not older)
was descended from James Sowerby, the famous scientist and botanical
illustrator. In fact there is no link whatsoever between the Tyneside Sowerbys
and the Lambeth Sowerbys. Several sources even referred to Githa as "Kate
Sowerby" and called her an artist and illustrator, presumably confusing her
with Millicent.

Githa was widely stated to have been born in Northumberland, when in fact
she was born in Gateshead, County Durham. Despite her Tyneside roots I
found that none of Githa's plays, including *Rutherford & Son,* had ever been
performed there, and even the National Theatre appeared not to know that

Githa had already had 11 children's books published by the time she wrote *Rutherford & Son*. *The Policeman's Whistle* was said to have been Githa's last play but in fact she had written a later one, *Direct Action*, around 1937-1938. And Githa was steeped in the philosophy and political thought behind the Arts & Crafts Movement, with which her father John George Sowerby had been closely associated.

I first met Githa's daughter, Joan Smith, now 91 years old, in April 2008 through the kind offices of Paul Taylor, the Performing Rights Director at Samuel French & Co. We found we have the same sense of humour and quickly became friends, sharing many a sandwich and glass of wine. Whenever I visited Joan at her elegant London apartment, we talked about anything and everything and every now and again, when we felt like it, we talked about Githa.

Joan initially felt she would have little to offer in my search for information about her mother, as Githa had delegated much of her daughter's care to a nanny. She was sad that her relationship with her mother had not been as close as she wished and, when I suggested that she and I should search for her mother together, she agreed immediately. In the course of our search, Joan found out a lot about her mother that she hadn't previously known, but she also found that she already knew a great deal more about her than she originally thought. It was no substitute for the close mother-daughter relationship that Joan had longed for when Githa was alive but I believe she feels a little closer to her mother as a result of our search. In any case, we have formed a friendship that will outlast this work we have done together.

My search took a great leap forward when, on 30 April 2008, I visited Joan in her flat and she showed me a hatbox full of memorabilia. When I say a hatbox, I don't mean a box that had originally contained a tiny confection of wire and net. This was a majestic hatbox that must once have housed an Ascot hat of immense proportions. It was a hatbox with such a sense of its own importance that one almost felt the need to curtsey before venturing to open it, and it was so heavy it took considerable strength to drag it across the floor towards my chair so that I could examine its contents properly. To my utter amazement, inside it I found the original scripts of all Githa's plays, including the fragile original prompt copy of *Rutherford & Son*, covered with Githa's handwritten comments, showing cuts that had been made in rehearsal. There was a large file of business correspondence between Githa and her agents Curtis Brown, including two letters to Githa from Harley Granville Barker, and a personal letter from Charles Brookfield, Examiner of Plays for the Lord Chamberlain's Office. There were original play programmes for *Rutherford & Son* (1912), *A Man and Some Women* (1914),

Sheila (1917), and *The Stepmother* (1924). There were production photographs of *Rutherford & Son* and *Sheila*, a stack of newspaper cuttings reviewing Githa's plays, and a few cuttings about her and her husband, John Kaye Kendall. And there was the script of a play called *Direct Action*. *Direct Action?* Could this be a play that no one knew Githa had written? Yes, it could, and it was.

There were very few family photographs. Joan explained that in 1931, when Githa's mother died, the family solicitor settling the estate had without authority sent the historic Sowerby family photograph album out to Canada to Githa's elder brother Lawrence, who had emigrated there in 1912. After Githa died in 1970, contact had been lost between the Canadian and English branches of the Sowerby family, and Joan was convinced that Lawrence's sons would probably have thrown the family album away long ago. As Tom and Eric had grown up in the wilderness of British Columbia, she felt they would have had no interest whatsoever in keeping a record of the Sowerby family history, even though both boys had been born in England.

Joan also explained that my search for information about her mother would be particularly difficult because shortly before she died in 1970, Githa had destroyed all her personal letters and family photographs. She had become convinced over the years that neither the public nor members of her own family were interested in her work or her achievements. Joan had been deeply upset by this but by the time she found out what her mother had done it was too late: everything was gone.

Despite the obvious difficulties in these circumstances of any search for information about Githa Sowerby, I became increasingly angry at the injustice done to this feminist playwright and children's author and felt I must do something about it. Githa had been so effectively obliterated from British theatrical history that not even her own family knew much about her background or realised how significant her work was. But looking for Githa was going to demand a lot of lateral thinking. I began to collect all Githa's children's books, all the children's books for which her father, John George Sowerby, had provided illustrations, the books by her cousin Murray Levick, and any books I could find about Sowerby glass. I read poetry by Githa's husband John Kaye Kendall, biographies of early 20th century theatrical figures such as Cicely Hamilton, Francesco Paolo Tosti and Harley Granville Barker; Lena Ashwell's autobiography, books of Victorian theatre criticism, Ray Strachey's wonderful history of the women's movement *The Cause*, Cicely Hamilton's damning 1909 book *Marriage as a Trade*, and Edward R Pease's fascinating 1916 *History of the Fabian Society*.

Over the next year with Joan's permission I carefully transported the contents of the hatbox to my home, where I preserved the documents in archive conditions. Sometimes on my regular visits to Joan we talked randomly about her mother and just enjoyed each others' company. At other times I sent Joan a list of topics I thought we could talk about on my next visit, so that she could have some reminiscences ready when I arrived. Joan, who at the start had thought she would have little information to give me, found she could remember a lot more than she thought. When I asked what Githa had done during the First World War, Joan told me of her mother's work as a volunteer in the Kensington War Supplies Depot. When I asked about their circle of friends, Joan reminisced about all the artists, actors and writers who had been regular guests at their house. Joan described vividly her visits to her great-aunt and great-uncle's house in Gloucestershire, Toddington Manor, and how frightened she had always been of the stained glass window there that depicted heaven and hell. She recounted to me what her mother had said about her privileged but miserable childhood and the coldness of her mother towards her. When Joan got to know me better she shared her hurt and anger about Githa's controlled and controlling personality, and she described the damage that this had done to their relationship as mother and daughter.

Joan joyfully reminisced about her father, to whom, in contrast, she had been very close. She told many stories that showed how the marriage of her parents had been a relationship of opposites, but a very happy relationship nonetheless. She talked about her cousins, including Antarctic explorer Murray Levick and award-winning sculptress Ruby Levick. She remembered what her cousin Barbara had told her about the suicide of another young cousin, Hugh Green, and how it had been hushed up to safeguard the social position of Githa's eldest sister Helen and her eminent clergyman husband.

I worked on the genealogical research into Sowerby family history in partnership with Tom Cruikshanks (a family history researcher related to the Tyneside Sowerbys by marriage) and I shared our findings regularly with Joan. I checked births, marriages and deaths while Tom checked Sowerby wills and property records, and we shared the task of searching the census returns. I contacted Githa's literary agents Curtis Brown and Samuel French & Co to ask for sight of their early files of correspondence with Githa, but it proved a dead end: once more I found that all the early documents had been destroyed.

In the autumn of 2008 I contacted Leila Muldrew of the Victoria Genealogical Society of British Columbia and asked if she could help us find the descendants of Githa's elder brother, Lawrence. Knowing that Lawrence's wife Lucy had died in the Sidney area of Vancouver Island in 1975, I also contacted Catherine George, a reporter from the *Peninsula News* there, and asked for the paper's help.

Both responded with enthusiasm to the task. The search for the Canadian branch of the Sowerby family took more than three months but in early 2009, with Leila and Catherine's help, we finally found Lawrence's grand-daughter and great-grand-daughter. 200 emailed historic Sowerby family photographs later, I was able to visit Joan with the prints, and restore to Githa's descendants the heritage they had lost in 1931. The two halves of the Sowerby family were once more in contact, to the mutual joy of the families on both sides of the Atlantic.

In September 2009, Lawrence's grand-daughter Joan Jolley and his great-grand-daughter Shannon will come to England to meet Githa's daughter Joan and their other English relatives. They will visit Tyneside for the festival to be held in honour of Githa Sowerby's work, and together will see the first ever production of *Rutherford & Son* on Tyneside. It is a joint production between Richard Beecham's Threshold Theatre and Newcastle's Northern Stage, and will have a genuine Tyneside cast of actors. There will be no more nonsense about the action being set in North Yorkshire.

When I first set out to look for Githa Sowerby almost two years ago, I had no thought of writing a book, but now *Looking for Githa* is being launched in September 2009 as part of that festival. The archive Joan Smith and I built up will go on permanent loan into the care of the Tyne & Wear Museum Service; thanks to the work of a local history society, the recently discovered graves of Githa's grandparents, John and Anne Sowerby, at St James's Church, Benwell, will be protected from future neglect (alongside neighbouring graves), and a blue plaque commemorating Githa Sowerby's achievements is about to be unveiled by Gateshead Council. Once this book is published it will no longer be true to say that "Little is known of Githa Sowerby..." She is at last being recognised as one of the most significant authors to have been born on Tyneside.

Pat Riley
Leeds, June 2009

CHAPTER ONE

The Curtain Rises

On the afternoon of 31 January 1912, John H Leigh, manager of London's Royal Court Theatre, presented the debut of a new work, *Rutherford & Son* by KG Sowerby, as part of his matinee programme of new plays. As a first time playwright, Sowerby was not a name London audiences would recognise, but the performance was an immediate hit. *Rutherford & Son* gave a new twist to the family drama, including a story-line about a sexual relationship between a glassworks foreman and the daughter of the owning family. Audiences were gripped by the story of the domestic tyrant John Rutherford, who judges the worth of everyone against their relevance to the profits to be made by his huge glassworks, driving his children one by one to flee his house and his ambition, only to meet his match at last in his courageous working-class daughter-in-law.

"One of the very best, strongest, deftest, and altogether most masterly family dramas that we have had for a long time from anyone, however famous," raved the reviewer for the *Daily Chronicle*. A "most powerful and arresting work," said the *Morning Post*; the dialogue was "tense and rings true, while the characters are keenly observed and successfully drawn". The writer for the *Manchester Guardian* summed it up. The audience had seen the debut of what was "clearly an author of first importance".[3] It was only when 'KG Sowerby' did not appear through the curtains to acknowledge the cries of "Author! Author!" that the reviewers realised that the wonderfully talented Mr Sowerby was not a mister at all. This starkly powerful drama had been written by a woman.

The woman in question was 35-year-old Katherine Githa Sowerby, known to family and friends as Githa, named by her father after a Saxon princess because of her beautiful light auburn hair. Very early the morning following her play's triumphant debut, she crept out of the Chelsea flat she shared with two of her sisters to buy copies of all the morning editions. On street corners, billboards screeched their message to the world with headlines such as 'FAME IN A DAY'. Githa persuaded a news vendor to let her have a poster that read 'COURT THEATRE: NEW AUTHOR'S REMARKABLE TRIUMPH'. She had it backed with linen to make sure it did not deteriorate and kept it as a life-long keepsake. As she walked along the deserted embankment that winter morning clasping her reviews, Githa thought that she could never again be as happy as she was at that moment. She confided as much to her cousin Gwen Levick later in the day as, huddled round the fire in the flat, they read and relished every single word the critics had written about *Rutherford & Son.*

Githa was not particularly happy about the theatre omitting her first name from the programmes and playbills but she could see the point. Experience taught that plays known beforehand by the critics to have been written by women received a bad press. If her play was to get a fair hearing, Githa's gender had to be concealed. *Rutherford & Son* was definitely not something theatre critics would expect a "womanly woman" to write about.

Despite such concerns, *Rutherford & Son* went from strength to strength. The publishing house Sidgwick & Jackson rushed to publish the script, gleefully quoting extracts from reviews on the dust-jacket[4]. There were only four matinee performances scheduled at the Royal Court Theatre, but Curtis Brown, Githa's literary agents, keen to build on the play's triumphant debut, swiftly made arrangements with actor-producer Charles Kenyon to transfer *Rutherford & Son* to popular actress and suffragist Gertrude Kingston's Little Theatre. Opening there on 18 March, its success continued unabated until, still under the production management of Charles Kenyon, the play transferred to the larger Vaudeville Theatre on 22 April. It remained at that theatre for the rest of the season. By the time it closed, *Rutherford & Son* had run for a total of 133 performances.

The audience treated the opening at the Vaudeville Theatre on 22 April as a first night all over again. This time Githa appeared through the curtains to acknowledge the applause personally but by now she was finding her new fame difficult to live with. The simple happiness of 1 February had been overtaken by a constant battle to cope with the number of journalists who wanted to interview this extraordinary new phenomenon, a woman playwright whose work was being compared to that of Ibsen. Many were the disgruntled critics who found their telephone messages responded to by "a deputy" (probably one of her sisters). When Githa did grant interviews, journalists were often taken aback by her responses to their questions. Though invariably charming and polite, she was cool, matter-of-fact and at times almost monosyllabic. They had to probe to get any significant answers out of her at all.

One of the first journalists to track Githa down was Keble Howard, a reporter for the *Daily Mail.* Howard was struck by the contrast between Githa's conventionally feminine appearance on the one hand and her starkly powerful playwriting on the other.

> "This new dramatist, about whom half the play-going world is talking, is just the sort of young Englishwoman that you may meet by the score

on tennis lawns or up the river. Tall, fair, with a pretty face and a very pleasant voice, you might suspect her of eating chocolates and talking nonsense in the shade, but you would never dream that she could be the author of a play with the grim force of a Pinero in the story or the sureness of a Galsworthy in the characterisation."[5]

Keble Howard pressed the new playwright as to the source of her finely drawn characters. Githa murmured that she had spent most of her "flapperhood" in Northumberland and, shielding her face from the heat of the fire with her muff, she continued:

"I'm awfully sorry but I haven't any ideas about my characters at all. Sometimes at rehearsal, my producer, Mr Foss, would ask me what some line or other meant. I couldn't tell him. Why should I know any more about them than anyone else? There they are, walking about and saying all these things. That's really all I know about them!"

Deliberately adding to the journalist's stereotype of the type of young woman who would spend her time eating chocolates and talking nonsense in the shade, Githa went on to deplore the fact that her characters had been so horrid to one another. Adding a finishing touch to the picture, she added that she had written most of the play in pencil in a notebook sitting in a boat on the river. It is small wonder, perhaps, that the final paragraph of Keble Howard's column is headed 'An Exasperated Interviewer!'

Keble Howard had met his match in Githa but another journalist caught a glimpse of the intellect behind the mask. Phil Farnum, who managed to get an interview with Githa soon after the premiere of *Rutherford & Son*, made the initial mistake of seeing her before he had read or seen her play. He started by asking if she had written "a love drama or the plot of an adventure". "Neither," Githa replied with a patient smile. "And I prefer that you should read it rather than that I should discuss it!"

Duly reproved and having talked to Githa further on a more adult level, Farnum discovered that she was no newcomer to the literary scene. Working with her illustrator sister, Millicent, she had had 11 children's books published since 1906. Githa Sowerby was therefore no *ingénue*; she was a self-supporting single woman. The journalist became genuinely interested in her career so far and asked how she had chanced to write a play after so many children's books. "I don't know," said Githa, for once drawn into giving more detail.

"I just thought I would write one and I had finished two acts when my friends, learning about it, supplied all kinds of discouragement. They said that before I could think of any measure of success in the dramatic field I must know all about stage techniques – the exits and entrances, the wings, and scenery. They said I was going against all traditions of the drama and that it was a waste of time for an amateur to try to prepare a production that could stand the glare of the footlights. And so the two acts went into a drawer for a time. Then by good chance I met a charming actress[i] who afterwards assumed a role in *Rutherford & Son* and she encouraged me by all means to finish the play. This I did, and it was produced."

Having concluded his interview, Farnum went away, looked at some of the children's books Githa had written and read *Rutherford & Son*. He was amazed at the strength of the writing. Having described *Rutherford & Son* in his column as "the most powerful play produced in England in a decade", he summed up Githa's achievement.

> "The truth is that the English people have in Miss Sowerby a positive genius, who has begun early but not abnormally, and who gives abundant evidence that she is destined to take rank with the world's best latter-day writers and thinkers."[6]

Githa's pose as an *ingénue* was successful in putting interviewers off the scent. She was not just a talented author – she was a talented actress too. In point of fact there was much to find out about where the idea for the overbearing northern glass manufacturer and his shattered family had come from, if only the journalists had seen through what many interpreted as Miss Sowerby's wide-eyed innocence. Githa never mentioned the northern town of her birth. She had been born into a wealthy dynasty of Gateshead glass manufacturers who had at one time been the leading makers of pressed glass in Europe, and, through the efforts of her father, John George Sowerby, had made a name for the production of superb stained and art glass.

---

i This actress was Thyrza Norman, who created the part of Mary Rutherford in the first production of *Rutherford & Son*. Norman was at first the ward and then wife of theatre manager JH Leigh who staged *Rutherford & Son* at his Royal Court Theatre in 1912.

CHAPTER TWO

Sowerby Glass

Glassmaking ruled the lives of the Tyneside Sowerbys for more than one hundred years. The family may even have been involved in glassmaking before the dawn of the 19th century, but there is no definite documentary evidence to support this. What is known, however, is that in the early 1800s the sons of Netherton gentleman farmer John Sowerby (1750-1843) and his wife Abigail (born Gillespy) were looking beyond the trees and fields of their native Cumberland to a different life. George Sowerby (1774-1844), his brothers Richard (1785-1811) and Thomas (1790-1863) and their brother-in-law John Phillips (husband of their sister Elizabeth, born in 1778), looked to make their fortunes amid the fumes and factories on the banks of the Tyne, where their distant cousin, Cuthbert Ellison MP, could ease their entry into the local economy.

As the first step towards a new life, Githa's great-grandfather, George, bought Shipcote Farm near Gateshead and moved his family there, while his brother Richard became a partner in a new glassworks being set up on land at Pipewellgate nearby. The factory was eventually named the New Stourbridge Glass Works, as two of the partners, James Robertson and John Seager, had been established glassmakers in the Midlands before moving to Gateshead. As historian Simon Cottle describes, the glassworks were situated:

> "... at the west end of Pipewellgate about a quarter of a mile from the Tyne Bridge... This meant that the works were close to the centre of the important port of Newcastle, the river offering enormous potential for distribution of their products around Britain and Europe."[7]

When Richard Sowerby died in 1811 aged just 26, the original partnership was dissolved and a new partnership replaced it, this time including Githa's great-grandfather George. Although George continued to farm and by 1812 had also bought a coalmine, from that time on the future of the Sowerby family on Tyneside became principally bound up with glassmaking. In 1816 the partnership running the New Stourbridge Glass Works was again changed to include George's brother Thomas and his brother-in-law John Phillips, who had both by now also moved from Cumberland to Gateshead and had established themselves as timber merchants on the other side of the Tyne in Newcastle.

The Sowerbys were skilful at creating alliances that would benefit the glassworks and consolidate the Sowerby family's commercial and political position in the town. Apart from Cuthbert Ellison, their business contacts included the influential Swinburne family. The initial input from the experienced Midlands glassmakers was crucial for the success of the venture. The New Stourbridge Glass Works became so successful that soon American competitors were complaining, alleging that to be able to price their goods so low the Tyneside manufacturers must be "defrauding the Revenue".[8]

Soon Githa's great-grandfather was making a great deal of money and was becoming a person of importance in Gateshead. No longer content with the basic accommodation provided at Shipcote Farm, he moved his family into the more impressive Shipcote House. Both farms were near enough to Pipewellgate to make his attendance there as easy as it had been from Shipcote Farm, and he settled down in his new house to run both farms and raise a family.

In 1806, before he moved to Gateshead, George Sowerby married Martha Wilson. The couple had five children, two of whom did not survive to adulthood. Martha herself died in 1828. Their eldest son John (1808-1879), Githa's grandfather, however, was strong in body and mind. He proved to be a businessman of extraordinary and precocious talent. He was to become the driving force behind the company's success.

There is some debate about how old Githa's grandfather was when he went to work at the New Stourbridge Glass Works. According to Simon Cottle in *Sowerby: Gateshead Glass*[9], John started work there in 1820 when he would have been only 12 years old. However, other authorities doubt this and believe he must have been older, as the family would surely have wanted to see that John received an adequate education before entering the glassworks. There is, however, no dispute about the fact that by the age of 24, John Sowerby was running the company with the help of his younger brother George (1822-1872), leaving their father free to pursue a political career in Gateshead.

Politics suited Githa's great-grandfather's competitive instincts. In 1835 he was elected to the Town Council. He was elected again in 1839 and in 1841 he became Mayor. In this capacity he made an address on behalf of the town to Queen Victoria on the occasion of the birth of her son and was made an Alderman. Soon afterwards, however, his health began to decline. He decided he no longer wanted the burden of running the farms at Shipcote. His final move was to a cottage in Chester-le-Street called Whitehill, where he lived until his death there in 1844.

In due course, as befitted his own success, Githa's grandfather, John Sowerby, moved to Benwell Towers, across the Tyne in Newcastle. Benwell Towers was certainly impressive and, though it was not particularly comfortable as a family home, it remained in the Sowerby family for a generation.

George's only surviving daughter Mary Anne, as was the custom, remained at home after her mother's early death to run the household: she did not marry until after her father died. By that time, George's heir, Githa's grandfather, was facing major financial problems if the New Stourbridge Glass Works were to continue to lead the market at home and abroad. The business was seriously in debt and when George Sowerby's will was proved in 1845, his effects were valued at under £1,000. Because of the importance of coal to the production of glass, Githa's great-grandfather had purchased the Waldridge coal mine using finance raised from a mortgage granted by the local bank run by the five Backhouse brothers and their partner, Jonathan Richardson. The same bank also held the overdraft for the New Stourbridge Glass Works. By the time George died, the company had accumulated debts of £41,794 to this bank – a large debt now but a huge one in 1844.

The Backhouse brothers were a constant irritant to Githa's grandfather. Their priority was to safeguard the banks' money and they knew nothing of the business of glass manufacture.

Knowing that a rival glassworks nearby was in trouble, John Sowerby covertly supported the members of the Glass Blowers Union there in a dispute with their employer over pay, even going as far as to undertake a court action against his rival for alleged intimidation of his workforce. His tactics paid off. The rival owner went bankrupt and John Sowerby was able to purchase his glassworks relatively cheaply. He set up a second company, The Gateshead Stamped Glass Works, at his new premises and there he experimented with the mechanisation of the glassmaking process.[10] He hired Samuel Neville, formerly manager of the Stourbridge glass company Bacchus & Green, to manage the new company, taking him into partnership alongside his own younger brother George Sowerby. But John did not in the end profit from his ruthless business tactics. The Glass Blowers Union began a pay dispute with him too and he was forced to sell the company he had only just acquired. The Gateshead Stamped Glass Works had to close[11] as a result.

Despite this setback, Githa's grandfather was confident that there were huge profits to be made if only he could find a way to make attractive glassware available cheaply to a mass market for the first time. To achieve this he needed to build a more modern and larger factory turning out glass through mechanised production processes. He secured the lease of more land in

Gateshead not far from Pipewellgate and by 1852 opened the much larger
Ellison Glass Works. He and Samuel Neville imported 50 glassmakers and
their families from the Midlands on a specially chartered train to work at
the new factory alongside the locally recruited workforce.[12] The immigrants
formed a small community beside the glassworks in a street of houses built by
the company. The London and North Eastern Railway extended a spur line
on to the company's land to facilitate distribution of the glassware and the
delivery of raw materials to the site. The Backhouse Bank, however, refused
to extend the overdraft of the original New Stourbridge Glass Works, forcing
John to sell it. Frustrated and angry, he determined to rid himself of the
Backhouse brothers. By selling his interest in the Waldridge coalmine (which
had never in any case been as profitable an investment as had been hoped)
he raised the funds to wipe out his debts to the bank. From that time on,
with the help of his younger brother George and glassworks manager Samuel
Neville, Githa's grandfather could run his business as he pleased.

The decision to lease the five and a half acres of additional land from
Cuthbert Ellison, to build a new factory equipped with modern machinery
and to move families from the Midlands to Gateshead to settle in houses
built by the company, had been an enormous gamble but it quickly paid off.
The Sowerby's Ellison Glass Works transformed the production of glassware
on Tyneside. Githa's grandfather set up offices in London, Paris and
Hamburg and his younger brother George became an agent for the company,
travelling frequently between these offices. With the competitive advantage
brought by mechanisation, the company became European market leader
in the sales of pressed glass and continued to compete successfully with its
American rivals.

Githa's grandfather was ruthless, ambitious and single-minded with no
time for sentiment. It seems that, like her great-grandfather, he was heavily
built with large shoulders, and kept himself physically fit. John Sowerby was
a keen mountain climber who climbed in the Alps with fellow members
of the Alpine Club as well as in Britain. From 1852 onwards, John always
wore a silk hat and frock coat when at the Glass Works but his men knew
that, despite his elegant clothes, he could still match any of them in physical
strength.[i] One story tells of how he shamed his men into ending a strike by
stripping to the waist and shovelling one and a half times more coal into the
furnaces than any of his employees could manage. He was much respected by
his workforce and in the town.

---

i John Sowerby's silk hat and frock coat were on show at the glassworks until 1949, long after it
had been taken over by Suntext, but it appears they have since been lost.

By now Githa's grandfather was a magistrate and a member of the Gateshead Board of Guardians (the local administrators of the Poor Law). In 1854 he and Samuel Neville were appointed to the jury of the official inquiry into a disastrous fire that had begun in a worsted factory on Gateshead quayside and spread to an adjoining chemical warehouse. Though the cities of Newcastle and Gateshead had united in trying to control the fire they were unsuccessful and an explosion of such violence occurred that it was heard by workers deep underground at Monkwearmouth colliery 11 miles away. The fire spread through nearby premises and large amounts of quayside property were destroyed. The inquiry went on for months and was adjourned many times. Eventually the jury, of which John Sowerby had been appointed foreman, determined that the explosion had been caused by nitrate of soda and sulphate reacting together either mechanically or accidentally. They recommended these two substances should not in future be stored or deposited near to each other[13].

Back in November 1842, Githa's grandfather had married Anne Robson, daughter of Daniel Robson,[14] one of his former neighbours when the family was living at Shipcote Farm. Over the next 14 years, John and Anne had six children – the five who would later become Githa's aunts and uncle: Isabella, known as Bella (born 1843), Martha, known as Mattie (born 1845), Jane, known as Jeannie (born 1847), Annie, known as Nan (born 1852), and Charles (born 1857). Their eldest son John George, Githa's father, was born in 1849.

Just as his own father George had done in the previous generation, John Sowerby regarded his children as an investment. His sons John George and Charles were raised to follow in his footsteps and take over the company, just as he and his brother George had been. His girls would be married to men whose wealth or social position could benefit the glassworks. Though this sounds barbaric to 21st century ears, it was commonplace among manufacturing families at that time to look for a return from the investment made in their children, in the same way a businessman would look for gain from any other kind of transaction. The practice was as prevalent on Tyneside as it was everywhere else in the country.

Nowhere was this strategic marketing of his daughters more successful for the Sowerby glass manufacturing empire than with the marriage John secured for his eldest daughter Isabella. In 1863 Bella married Hugh Andrews, a wealthy Belfast ship-owner who also owned coal mines. A shrewd, if irascible, businessman, Andrews was a significant catch and to celebrate the union John gave a dinner at the Queen's Hotel, Gateshead, to which 150 guests were invited.[15] Hugh Andrews became a close ally first of his father-in-law, then of his brother-in-law John George, Githa's father, when Sowerby's Ellison Glass Works became a limited company in 1881. Eventually he would become chairman of the Sowerby board. He had the Midas touch and when he died in 1926, left an estate of almost £500,000, which in terms of its purchasing power in the early 21st century would amount to many millions.

John forged his next alliance with the marriage of his daughter Mattie in 1869 to up-and-coming barrister and aspiring politician Francis William MacLean. In the short-term the marriage brought increased social standing for the Sowerbys but it had even greater potential as Francis William MacLean was a rising star. As it happened, MacLean's major political successes came after John's death in 1879 – after becoming MP for Woodstock (1885-1891), the then Sir Francis was appointed Lord Chief Justice of Bengal from 1896 to 1909.

In 1870 John married his daughter Jane, known as Jeannie, to George Levick, the second son of Frederick Levick of the company Levick & Simpson. Levick & Simpson had formerly owned massive ironworks at Blaina and Coalbrooke Vale in Monmouthshire, employing more than 5,000 people.[16] The moulds for pressed glass were made of iron, so the metal was of great importance to glass manufacture. A will drafted by Frederick Levick in 1858 shows the wealth of the Levick family before the market for Welsh iron ore began to suffer from competition from cheaper and purer Spanish iron ore. In 1858 Frederick Levick expected to leave his various beneficiaries a large house, shares in his two companies, carriages, horses, china, glass, furniture, pictures, linen, household goods, provisions, and large sums of money. However, in the mid-1860s, Levick & Simpson crashed with huge debts. By the time of his death in 1867, Frederick Levick, an honourable businessman held in high esteem by his employees and the local community, had paid off those debts in full. But when his will was proved in 1869, his estate was valued at under £200. His unmarried daughters had to leave Wales and find work as school-teachers and governesses, while his second son, George, began working independently as a civil engineer. Only his eldest son, Frederick, remained at Blaina, having been appointed as a consultant to the company that had taken over the ironworks from Levick & Simpson.

It seems surprising in these circumstances that Githa's grandfather permitted Jeannie's marriage to George Levick to take place. Perhaps it was simply that, as George Levick's brother Frederick was still employed at Blaina, John Sowerby saw an opportunity to cement a relationship with a potentially useful business contact. Favourable relations with the ironworks at Blaina meant John could avoid dependency on the much smaller Tyneside ironworks companies for his iron supplies. However, the fact that – unlike all her sisters

– no wedding photograph of Jeannie survives, suggests that John Sowerby was not as committed to this match as he was to the commercially and socially profitable marriages he arranged for his other daughters.

After their wedding, George and Jeannie Levick went to live at Blaina but in 1876, just before their son George Murray Levick was born, they moved back to Newcastle. Given the Victorian convention that daughters returned home for the birth of their first child, it seems strange that they did not return to the North East earlier. According to the UK censuses in 1881, 1891 and 1901, there were two earlier children born to George and Jeannie Levick at their home in Wales – Ruby Winifred, born around 1872, and Lorna Gwenllyan (known as Gwen, who became one of Githa's closest friends), born around 1874. But there is no trace of a birth registration under these names at this time, either at the local Register Office in Blaina or in the national records at the General Register Office. It was against the law not to register births and it seems most unlikely that George and Jeannie would have broken the law. The only logical conclusion seems to be that the births of both girls had already been registered but elsewhere and under other names. If so, Ruby and Gwen were not the natural children of the union between George and Jeannie Levick, despite being brought up as their daughters.

Why they were adopted[i] and who Ruby and Gwen Levick actually were, is unknown. But Gwen, who was a violinist by profession, had red hair like Githa's. Ruby was an outstandingly talented painter and sculptress. Given the known artistic talent of members of the Sowerby family, it is possible that Ruby and Gwen were the illegitimate children of one of the Sowerby men but were brought up as the children of George and Jeannie Levick to protect them from the stigma of illegitimacy. When Jeannie's son George Murray Levick died, his obituary in *The Times* described him as an only child[17]. However, *The Times* is unable to shed any light on the matter of Ruby and Gwen's parentage now. If Githa knew the truth of their origins, then that knowledge died with her. Unfortunately, there are no living descendants of George and Jeannie Levick who might have cleared up this mystery.

In 1875 Githa's grandfather matched his fourth daughter, Annie, with Henry Stewart Murray Graham (1849-1913), a member of another well connected family, this time from the Scottish aristocracy. Henry Stewart Murray Graham's seat was Murrayshall. Graham inherited this mansion in Kinnoull, Perthshire, with its 1,913 acres of land in 1881. An impressive tombstone

---

i Legal controls on the process of adoption were not introduced into the UK until 1926, so an arrangement that George and Jeannie Levick were to bring up someone else's children as their own would have been a private affair with the details known only to the people involved.

erected to mark the death of Henry Stuart Murray Graham in the cemetery at Balgowan commemorates him with his wife, Anne, and describes him as a distinguished Colonel in the Royal Artillery.

John's sons were raised as a matter of course to take over Sowerby's Ellison Glass Works, but John's youngest son, Charles, proved a disappointment. The first Sowerby to attend a fee-paying private school outside his home area[18], Charles was not attracted to the life his father had planned for him. He left home for pastures new before taking any part at all in the family business. There is no trace of Charles in the UK census of 1881 and his whereabouts for the 19 years from 1871 are unknown.

However, in 1893 Charles Sowerby applied to the authorities at Breckenridge, Colorado, for naturalisation as an American citizen. On his application form he stated that he had been in America since 1890. Breckenridge was the nearest town to the 1890 gold strike at Cripple Creek, so it seems likely that Charles went to America to prospect for gold. This is supported by the fact that by 1900, Charles, now a naturalised American, was still working as a miner, though by then in Cook County on the outskirts of Chicago, Illinois.[19] According to local records, Charles had married a woman 17 years his senior called Harriet Razey two years earlier in Jefferson County, Colorado.[20] It appears Charles wished Harriet to believe he was considerably older than he really was, since he added ten years to his real age when he gave his details to the US Federal Census in 1900. This may not have been a difficult subterfuge to carry off as the harsh life of a miner had clearly taken its toll.

Three months later in July 1900, Charles was dead at the early age of 43, the cause of death being recorded as mitral heart disease and cerebral thrombosis. What happened to Harriet is unknown and it is unclear whether Charles's parents or brother and sisters ever knew where he had gone after he left England. Money was placed in trust for him in the wills of his father in 1879 and of his mother in 1896 but it seems probable that he never knew of the death of his parents or received the bequests.

What Charles gave up in terms of material comforts, wealth and privilege when he chose to flee his destiny at the glassworks and seek his fortune abroad is apparent from the size of the Sowerby household. The 1871 census shows that Githa's grandparents employed eight resident servants at Benwell Towers – a butler, a footman, a lady's maid, a cook, a seamstress, a laundress, two housemaids and a kitchen-maid – and there would of course have been other non-resident staff employed in the house and on the estate. The census also reveals that at this time John Sowerby employed 750 people at the glassworks.

With the departure of Githa's uncle Charles from the scene, the Sowerby family's continuing control of the glassworks depended solely on John's remaining son John George, Githa's father. John George, who had been educated at the Royal Kepier Grammar School Houghton-le-Spring, entered the glassworks as manager and colour-mixer at the age of 22 in 1871. It was an opportune time to take over. Just a year previously, Sowerby's Ellison Glass Works had registered its trade mark of a peacock's head to protect its designs against the widespread piracy at home and abroad. The future looked promising. Although rival companies were catching up with the sophistication of the Sowerby operation, Githa's father seems to have begun his work there with great enthusiasm. He registered a number of patents to protect his innovations, including a new means of ornamenting glass in 1871 and in 1874 an improved form of press. He also set up a studio at the glassworks to experiment with the production of art glass.

John George Sowerby, who was very keen on physical fitness, was soon putting into practice some of his new ideas to improve working conditions for his employees. He encouraged the men to take up boxing and wrestling, two of his favourite sports. He provided gym equipment on site for his employees to improve the health of the workforce He also made an abortive attempt to set up a brass band. The band came to an abrupt end after a riotous night out when the inebriated members abandoned their instruments, which were found scattered in various locations around Newcastle the following morning.[21]

Githa's father was also a keen amateur oarsman. At the time, thanks to oarsman and designer Harry Clasper (1812-1870), the Tyneside area was at the forefront of the design and building of fast boats for competitive rowing. Regattas were held regularly several times a year and drew huge crowds to the Tyne, with many bets being placed on the outcome of the races. The occasions on which crews from the Thames area were beaten by crews from Tyneside caused particular excitement. The level of celebration rose to a peak when Tyneside produced two World Champions at single sculls – Bob Chambers (1831-1868) and James Renforth (1842-1871).[22] John George Sowerby was by no means in the top flight of oarsmen but he was a keen member of the Tyneside Amateur Rowing Club and in 1877 he "easily beat John Lowthian Bell…by nearly a third of a mile in a skiff race for a piece of silver plate valued at £50".[23]

In 1872 Githa's father married Amy Margaret Hewison, who brought an income of £900 a year from her deceased father, a Newcastle corn merchant. During the next ten years they had six children – John Lawrence (born 1873), Margaret Helen (born 1874), Katherine Githa (born 1876), Amy

Millicent (born 1877), Marjory Gladys (born 1880), and Rachel Ruth (born 1882). All the children except Marjory were known by their second names. Not long before Githa's birth in 1876, the family moved from 6 Windsor Terrace in Newcastle to Ravenshill, an impressive house on Low Fell. There John George and Amy Margaret lived well, employing seven resident servants – a nurse and an under-nurse, a housemaid[i] and an under-housemaid, a cook, a butler, and a kitchen-maid.

Githa's father was a talented landscape painter and a keen patron of the arts. When the work of a young marine and coastal painter, Thomas Marie Madawaska Henry, came to his notice, John George sent the young man at his expense to study drawing under Verlat in Antwerp. John George helped to arrange art exhibitions on Tyneside and submitted several of his own paintings for exhibition, both in London and locally. He became friendly with major figures in the art world and spent a great deal of time in London. Githa's grandfather was very critical of his eldest son's frequent trips to the capital, feeling he was neglecting his duties at the glassworks. However, John George was moderately successful in his artistic endeavours. Eventually he would have 13 of his pictures exhibited at the Royal Academy and nine works hung in other London exhibitions. His paintings are now considered very collectable, and many are American-owned.

At the end of the 1870s John George took up a part-time career as an illustrator of children's books. He published his first two books, *Come With Me* and *Afternoon Tea*, in 1880. These were followed by *At Home* in 1881, *At Home Again* in 1882, *Jimmy, Scenes from the Life of a Black Doll, As Told by Himself* in 1888, and *Young Maids and Old China* in 1889. He worked with various writers, the first for *Come With Me* being his brother-in-law, Frederick Hewison. For his later books John George collaborated with members of the Arts & Crafts Movement such as Walter and Thomas Crane, FW Bourdillon and Tyneside artist HH Emmerson. He was a close friend of Thomas Crane, elder brother of Walter. John George also worked with poet and children's author Eliza Keary.

For many of the illustrations in his early books, John George used his own young children – including Githa – as his models, and his luxurious Low Fell home, Ravenshill, as the setting. Through the books he illustrated both on his own and with others, John George Sowerby shared the lives of his children with the world. In *Afternoon Tea,* published in 1880 when Lawrence was seven, Helen was six, and Githa was four, there is an illustration which names

---

i The name of the housemaid was Mary Rutherford, which presumably is where Githa found the name for her character of Mary Rutherford in *Rutherford & Son.*

the children in the picture as Lawrence, Helen and Gisha [sic]. From this we can identify John George's three eldest children elsewhere in their father's books, even when in the accompanying poems they are given other names for the sake of the story.

John George's illustrations show his children copying the behaviour of their parents in their play. For example, in an illustration in *At Home,* Lawrence stands in front of the fireplace pretending to read a newspaper while one of his sisters plays mother, pouring tea at the breakfast table and asking her "husband" to tell her what is going on in the world. In another, *The Geography Lesson*, Githa plays the part of the governess in the schoolroom at Field House. In planning his children's books, John George and his collaborators were well aware of what Victorian middle-class parents expected. They wanted confirmation of their view of the world. Boys were to be raised to be fit for the rough world of business and wealth generation. They were to play competitive games, read adventure stories, and in due course be sent away to school to be educated, to learn self-reliance, and become gentlemen. In contrast, daughters were to remain at home learning accomplishments such as needlework, painting, and playing the piano, to equip them for eventual marriage when they would become the *Angels in the House*[ii] – gentle, self-sacrificing and deferential to their men-folk.

The female stereotypes held dear by Victorian society were comfortably reinforced in John George Sowerby's children's books. At the time Githa was born in 1876, middle-class women were still placed firmly in the domestic sphere. In most prosperous homes, girls were given a fair general standard of education but their delicate constitutions were thought too weak to sustain the intellectual demands of studying academic subjects and in any case such training was held to make girls less marriageable. Daughters were to be raised to fulfil as adults the roles of a calm and nurturing mother, a pure, loving and faithful wife, and a passive, delicate, and virtuous sister. They were to be ready at all times to put aside their own needs and wishes for the benefit of the men in the family. Women were supposed to be more spiritual beings than men and to preserve that natural soulfulness they needed to be protected, held in "a perpetual childhood" by their decision-making husbands and fathers.

Unsurprisingly, Githa's perception of her childhood does not match the idealistic picture of her father's picture books. John George's many illustrations depict Githa, Lawrence and Helen as carefree and happy –

---

ii *Angels in the House* is a long lyric poem published in its final form in 1862 by Coventry Patmore. The poet dedicated the work to his wife, whom he considered to be a model of Victorian womanhood.

playing horses, fishing, plotting to steal apples or catch unwary birds, trying to play Grandpa's cello, and pretending to be grown up. The sun seems to shine every day, the children's impractical clothes are always immaculate, their hair is always tidy and their faces and hands are clean. Given that for much of their childhood he saw little of his children, John George may not have known how far his pictures differed from daily life as his children lived it. His children led largely separate lives from their parents in nursery and school-room. John George Sowerby was an important figure at Sowerby's Ellison Glass Works, a member of one of the most powerful families in Gateshead, and roles in the Sowerby family were staunchly traditional. Father went daily to the glassworks, mother got up late and spent her days making social calls or occupied with her own affairs.

As a child Githa saw considerably less of her parents, and particularly of her mother, than Victorian text-books on child-rearing recommended. Her mother appears to have been neither loving nor demonstrative. Later in life, once, in anger, Githa accused her mother of being "faultily faultless, icily regular, splendidly null" – as beautiful and cold as Maud in Alfred Lord Tennyson's poem.[24] She believed her mother disliked her. Amy Margaret Sowerby kept Githa firmly at a distance and, since Nurse did not like her either, there was no one to show her any affection. In later years Githa remembered her childhood as bleak and unhappy, and the atmosphere at home as cold and oppressive.

Living almost separate lives from their parents in nursery wings at Ravenshill, Hall Garth and Field House, the quality of the lives of Victorian children like Githa and her brother and sisters depended largely on what kinds of people their nurses and governesses were. Just once a day, Amy Margaret Sowerby would call at the nursery to ask their Scottish nurse Mary Ann Clark if her young children had been good. It seems that she was always happy to hear bad reports of Githa. Nurse Clark, aware of this, invariably presented Githa as leading the others into trouble. "Well, madam, Miss Githa…" would be followed by a long list of misdemeanours Githa had allegedly committed in the course of each day. A particularly heinous crime occurred when, in the absence of Nurse at teatime, Githa spread a whole pot of strawberry jam on the children's bread and butter till none remained to be returned to the kitchen. Some mothers might have been privately amused by their child's boldness and leadership qualities, but not Amy Margaret Sowerby. Mama was not impressed, and efforts were redoubled to suppress Githa's headstrong spirit. Amy Margaret did not want an "unwomanly" daughter.

One of John George's illustrations shows a six-year-old Githa looking inside a grandfather clock. According to the poem that accompanies this picture, she takes hold of the pulley to see if stopping the clock ticking will stop time. (That this clock was part of the furniture inside John George Sowerby's luxurious home at Ravenshill is suggested by the peacock feathers above the portraits, echoing the trademark of Sowerby's Ellison Glass Works.) The illustration is testament to Githa's reputation as a child for getting into mischief. It also suggests that her father was aware of Githa's high intelligence (he must have realised that few six-year-olds would think of trying to see whether stopping clocks also stops time). Unfortunately for Githa, this awareness did not lead her father to consider giving her a better education than the basic teaching traditionally thought to be sufficient for Sowerby girls.

Githa felt her lack of proper education keenly throughout her life. She knew only too well what it felt like to take second place educationally to men. Her elder brother Lawrence, as the male heir to the Sowerby glassmaking dynasty, was educated at Winchester College. Unlike Lawrence, who loved competitive sport (particularly rowing and rifle shooting) and showed no academic potential whatsoever, Githa with her searing intelligence and intense interest in people, had to make do with the limited education a governess could offer for a few hours each morning in the schoolroom. Githa tried to make up for the deficiencies in her education by reading everything she could lay her hands on, but she never felt it was enough.

Although she had her brother and sisters for company, Githa found the isolation of their childhood frustrating. The grounds of Ravenshill on the slopes of Low Fell could only be reached by one of two footbridges and were cut off from the surrounding area. There were no other children to play with unless a family with children considered equal to theirs in social station came to stay. The Sowerbys were never allowed to play with local children. So instead Githa peopled the grounds with the children of the past. She imagined them emerging from the shadows to play with her, and hiding when Nurse came along in case they were sent to bed. She imagined the world beyond the footbridge as a place where enemies might live who would keep her and her brother and sisters prisoner if they were once to venture across it into the land beyond.[i]

Inevitably, wherever John George Sowerby walked, the shadow of his exceptional father followed him. Like many people who are young and want to do things differently, he was not popular with senior figures in the company, and his father's partner Samuel Neville left the glassworks when

---

i This fantasy later became the fairy story *Bumbletoes*, written by Githa, illustrated by Millicent, and published by Chatto & Windus in 1907.

John George took over in 1871. However, as Githa's grandfather maintained an active interest in the running of the glassworks until his death in 1879[25], John the Elder's experience and the respect in which he was still held no doubt helped Githa's father at least to begin to establish himself as a manager.

Unlike Githa's grandfather, her father was not a gifted entrepreneur. Thrift was foreign to his nature – he became famous among the men for throwing handfuls of gold sovereigns into the colour mixes to see what effect this would have on the design. His real talent was art and, apart from the design aspects and his great inventiveness in colour-mixing, John George had little enthusiasm for the routine production of pressed glass for the mass market. His ambition was to bring his company's products more in line with those of the art glass strongly favoured by his friends, many of whom were members of the Arts & Crafts Movement.

At some point, John George realised that his daughter Githa was different from her sisters and had gifts that could be useful to him in his business. From childhood, Githa was beautiful – tall for her age, slim and graceful, with a clear complexion and the thick light auburn hair that had inspired her father to name her after a Saxon princess. While she was still a child, John George began to send for his daughter to come down to the drawing-room in the evening to help entertain his guests. She hated her time spent in the company of his business guests and became increasingly desperate to avoid the ordeal. One evening she even emptied a large jug of water over her hair to escape, but it was to no avail. She was severely reprimanded for causing her parents embarrassment, and she still had to spend her evenings in the drawing-room whenever there were guests. John George was either unaware of Githa's distress or chose to ignore it, seeing it as her duty as his daughter to comply with his wishes. Her father's singling her out in this way not only made Githa unhappy, it cannot have endeared her to her sisters – especially Helen, who as the eldest daughter might reasonably have expected to be seen as first choice for this role. But Githa was the most suitable candidate and her father's choice was law.

However much Githa hated her evenings spent wholly in adult company, it was to this experience that she owed her grasp of the technicalities of the glassworks business which she was later to use to such good effect in writing *Rutherford & Son*. She heard her father and his colleagues discussing their battles with boards of directors and banks, the limitations of patent law, the effect on the glass business of strikes among the coal miners, the need for furnaces to reach a particular temperature if the firing is to be successful, and the use of muffle furnaces for experimental work in the creation of new metals[i] and colours. When the talk among the grown-ups turned to reminiscence, she heard tales of her grandfather and great-grandfather and how they had founded the firm and built it up from nothing. She would have heard excited talk about her father's exploits as an amateur oarsman. Perhaps, if the adults forgot there was a child present, she might even have eavesdropped on family secrets, such as the disappearance from the family of her uncle Charles. It was no doubt during those hours, when she had to smile and listen to please her parents, that Githa developed the rigid self-control that was to characterise her as an adult. She also learned without realising it the skills of observation and character analysis that would later stand her in such good stead as a dramatist.

As an adult Githa was ever conscious of how physically comfortable and privileged her upbringing had been compared with the lives of the young children who were forced through their parents' poverty to work in Gateshead's squalid quayside factories. Her father's personal political views are not on record but there is evidence that John George tried to be an enlightened employer. His provision of exercise facilities at the works to improve the health of his workforce was a real innovation for the time. And it was through her father that Githa would have first come across the work of the Fabian Society.

Various well-known Fabians were part of John George's circle at Ravenshill, Hall Garth and Field House. Because of John George's association with the Arts & Crafts Movement he would have known William Morris, who was a member of the Fabian Society. Walter Crane, with whom John George worked on his book *At Home,* was a prominent Fabian until he parted company with the Society over its attitude to the Boer war. Walter's elder brother Thomas was a regular visitor to the Sowerby household, as John George and he were close friends and often collaborated over book illustrations. There may well have been discussion in the Sowerby household about the activities of the Fabian Society when Githa was growing up, and she would have listened to talk of economics, politics and philosophy during her evenings spent in the drawing-room with her father's guests.

In 1879 Githa's grandfather died. Inevitably, his passing was a big loss to the Sowerby business. It was John's relentless drive and determination that had taken the company to the height of its success and the imprint of his personality was everywhere. It was open to question whether the momentum could possibly be maintained without him.

---

i In the glass-making industry, the word 'metal' is used as a slang description of glass. Thus, when young John Rutherford in the play *Rutherford & Son* says he has invented a new way of creating "white metal", he means he has invented a new way of making clear glass.

John Sowerby's will, proved in May 1879, two months after his death, provided for his wife and divided most of his property between his son-in-law Hugh Andrews and Githa's father. Separate bequests were made for each of his daughters, with Isabella Andrews' bequest at £24,000 being four times greater than that of any of her sisters. This no doubt reflected Githa's grandfather's debt to Hugh Andrews for his support since the marriage to his eldest daughter in 1863. The discrepancy between the size of their bequests, and the much greater sums given to Hugh Andrews and their brother John George, would not have surprised his three other daughters. For Githa's grandfather the future of the glassworks came before all, and men were more important than women. It was as simple as that.

Within a year of Githa's grandfather's death in 1879, her grandmother moved to London to be near to her daughters Bella Andrews, Mattie MacLean and Jeannie Levick. Bella and Mattie both had town houses in Kensington and main homes in the country while Jeannie, having far less money, had moved from Newcastle to modest accommodation at Acton in Middlesex with her husband and children. Because Jeannie's daughter Ruby, a gifted painter and sculptor, wished to attend art classes, she moved from Acton to live with her grandmother in Kensington in 1890. Ruby was eventually accepted at the National Art Training School (later the Royal College of Art), South Kensington, and studied there from 1893 to 1897. In 1895 Ruby was awarded the Queen's Medal (established in 1856) by the Science and Art Department and following this she won a British Institution scholarship for her modelling, and in addition the Princess of Wales scholarship. This was a ground-breaking achievement for a woman artist. It had not been long since the ban on women attending life drawing or life modelling classes for reasons of propriety had been lifted and their attendance at such classes was still very controversial. Ruby married architect Gervase Bailey in 1905 and, though she continued to paint and sculpt as a hobby, sadly she did not pursue a professional career. Ruby, too, was a close friend of Githa, though never as close to Githa as Ruby's sister Gwen.

Meanwhile, back on Tyneside, storm clouds were gathering. The decision was made in 1880 to turn Sowerby's Ellison Glass Works into a private limited company. John George was elected the first chairman of the board in 1881. He soon discovered that he no longer wielded anything like the power his father had. Githa's father had made a fatal error by not becoming one of the majority shareholders like his brother-in-law Hugh Andrews and the family solicitor, George Armstrong. Although his brother-in-law supported him, John George had enemies elsewhere, and he found it difficult to combat their influence.

Immediately after his father's death, John George had established two new limited companies – The Gateshead Stained Glass Company and The Gateshead Art Pottery – to produce high quality goods for niche markets. The implications of this new departure for the overall profitability of the company did not inspire confidence in the more conservative members of the board. Unfortunately, these board members were proved right. Neither of the new ventures was commercially successful, although they produced some products of great beauty including pieces inspired by the work of two Venetian glassmakers brought over by John George from Murano.

The new companies lost money and were relatively short-lived. Though no one doubted John George's abilities with art glass, colour-mixing and design, these failures raised serious questions about the quality of his commercial judgment. Despite sales of pressed glass reaching a record level in 1883, Githa's father was caught up in constant boardroom battles. He was finally driven to resign from the board in November 1883, and was succeeded as chairman by Hugh Andrews.

John George's loss of income led to his being declared bankrupt. He sold Ravenshill to settle his debts and moved his family to Hall Garth, a picturesque manor house he rented at Coatham Mundeville, in County Durham. The company must have missed John George's talent as a designer and colour-mixer, however, for five months later the board appointed him joint manager with another man, H Pitt, at a salary of £800 a year. Although he needed the income, it must have been a bitter pill to swallow for the former owner of the company and present minority shareholder to accept the role of a salaried member of the workforce.

John George's return to the company as joint manager did not go smoothly. His introduction into management at Sowerby's Ellison Glass Works had been in the days of his father's autocratic power. Attempts by the board to work out a compromise between John George and Pitt as joint managers proved doomed from the outset. The relationship between the two managers was poor, and problems between John George and some members of the board continued. Pitt was not popular with customers and there were justified complaints of poor quality products, but in 1887 Githa's father was forced to resign again, only to be reinstated as joint manager against much opposition in 1889 – by which time the company was in serious trouble.

This was John George's chance to rehabilitate himself with the board. He moved his family from Hall Garth back to Tyneside, renting Field House at High Teams in Gateshead, an impressive house with a 44 acre estate. Living nearer to the glassworks made Githa's father's attendance there easier and facilitated the provision of family hospitality to business contacts. Unfortunately, however, John George's commercial judgment was still questionable. The advice he gave for rescuing the company's market position – including the setting up of a new company to make bottles – did not help. The bottle company, too, was short-lived. By the time Githa's elder brother, Lawrence, went into the glassworks as a junior manager in 1890, their father was becoming thoroughly disillusioned. He began to take less and less interest in the company.

The family's happy years at Hall Garth had given John George a taste of life away from the domination of the glassworks. He had been able to spend more time painting and to indulge his interest in the natural world, making detailed observations of the wildlife that abounded on the 70 acre estate. By 1890 John George was longing to leave the glassworks behind so that he might live as a full-time artist. Like a prisoner about to escape from gaol, he made ready to hand over to a younger substitute who could carry the torch on behalf of the Sowerby name. For three generations in Gateshead, the Sowerbys had enjoyed power, money and privilege in abundance, but the price had been high. They had lived in households where the women of the family were all but invisible and the men's hearts had pumped blood only to maintain the roar of the furnaces. But, unbeknownst to his father, resourceful outdoors man Lawrence had other dreams; dreams that did not include devoting his life to Sowerby's Ellison Glass Works.

As John George's involvement at the glassworks dwindled, his financial difficulties mounted. Githa's father had long ago exhausted the money left to him by his father in 1879. When Sowerby's Ellison Glass Works became a limited company in 1881, John George's decision not to become one of the two majority shareholders had not only robbed him of personal power in the company, it had also reduced his income considerably. Now that John George's children were growing up, the household could maintain its former standard of living with half the number of resident domestic servants the family had previously had to employ[26] but he was feeling the pinch financially. Fed up with the endless boardroom battles, in 1894 he gave up the rental of Field House and moved the family once more out of Gateshead, to a property referred to in surviving documents as Chollerton House, near Hexham in Northumberland.[27]

In 1896, Anne Robson Sowerby, Githa's grandmother, who had moved back to the North East from London, died. Her estate after tax realised less than £15,000 and, as she divided it between her six children, the resulting benefit to John George was not great. At the same time Lawrence decided that five years as a glassworks manager (from 1890-1894) was more than enough.

In 1896 John George's heir left England for Africa to take up a post with the South African police, making it clear to his father that he would never return to the family business. Apparently with little thought for his own or his family's long-term financial stability, John George severed his connection with the glass works altogether by selling all his shares.[28] There was no energy, confidence or commitment to Grandfather Sowerby's cause left. If the furnaces of the Ellison Glass Works were still to be fed, then someone other than a Sowerby would have to do it.

CHAPTER THREE

Placing art above duty

The 1896 sale of John George Sowerby's shares in the glassworks changed everything for his family. By reinventing himself as a full-time artist, and turning his back on his role as wealth generator, the traditional structure of the family began to crumble. John George was no longer the archetypal Victorian father grappling daily with the competitive world of business and coming home each evening to be soothed by his loving family. Instead he spent his days doing what most Victorians regarded as a hobby – painting – while he lived on dwindling capital. As a result, although his wife, Amy Margaret, still confined herself to the traditional role of a wife, the ties of tradition on his daughters began to loosen.

Githa was at last set free from the drawing room evenings she so detested as there were no more business guests for her father to impress. He now spent all his time painting and observing wildlife locally. John George's final book, *Rooks and Their Neighbours,* published in 1895, chronicles his observations of rooks and other birds, starting with detailed notes he made during the family's time at Hall Garth. It is the only one of his books for which he supplied both the text and the illustrations. It is not a children's book. In it he frequently compares the lives of the rooks and their care of their chicks with the lives of parents caring for their children. Given the lack of sensitivity of some of his actions, his text shows an unexpected level of warmth and humanity – qualities he had no doubt had to suppress under the watchful gaze of boardroom colleagues in case they were interpreted as signs of weakness.

By 1899 John George developed some health problems and decided to take his family south, hoping his health might improve. Plans were made for a move to Boxted House near Colchester, a late Georgian house in a historic village on the Suffolk-Essex border. The move could not come soon enough for Githa, who at the age of 23 was utterly bored with life away from civilisation. She disliked the countryside and detested walking. She hated the emptiness and isolation of her existence. There were a few distractions in Northumberland; a few young people with whom she could socialise, but she was a restless character, desperately in need of intellectual stimulation. With the planned move to Essex, Githa would be closer to the artistic life of London. Removed from the shackles of Sowerby tradition, she would be one step nearer the life of an independent woman, which she longed for.

Boxted is a picturesque and historic village five miles from Colchester. It is situated in part of Dedham Vale, in 'Constable Country'. No doubt that is why landscape painter John George Sowerby chose this location in which to start his family's new life in the south of England. Though Githa's father was the first artist to choose the solid late Georgian Boxted House as a family home, he was not the last. In the 1930s the house became a meeting place for artists when it was owned by Natalie Bevan and her husband Lance Sieveking; for many years it housed a wonderful collection of modern art.

As John George had hoped, his health improved in the milder climate of the south. At Boxted he found himself in the midst of countryside much softer than the fells of Northumberland which, as a landscape painter, presented him with a whole new set of artistic challenges. Githa's father was in his element. He had finally escaped from the unfavourable comparisons that were constantly being made at the glassworks between himself and his more successful father. He was living as the artist he had longed to be. His relief was enormous, his sense of freedom overwhelming. For the rest of his life Githa's father wasted no energy thinking about the future. His thoughts were always of today and of his next picture. He decided that he would paint as many landscapes as inspired him in his new surroundings and when, in a few years' time, he felt the need of a new challenge he would simply move the family somewhere else. The cost implications of this plan, and the fact that his income was much lower than it had previously been, did not deter him. He was an artist and he would need to go to different places to paint his landscapes. To him that was the only relevant consideration.

With their father's attention absorbed in his art, the Sowerby children took advantage of their new-found freedom. Githa and her sisters were to be the first generation of Sowerby girls who would be free to choose to marry as they wished; the first generation who would not have to be put up for auction. After his year with the British South African Police (1896-1897), Githa's elder brother Lawrence moved to his own farm in Cumberland. Then, in 1900, her elder sister Helen announced her intention to marry. Helen's chosen partner was their 35-year-old cousin, the Reverend Reginald Southwell Graham Green, Rector of the parish of Croglin in Cumberland. He and Helen had known each other since childhood. Reginald was the son of their wonderfully named uncle Josephus Henry Green, husband of her mother's eldest sister Elizabeth Hewison.

Concerns were immediately raised by a number of family members at the possible medical risks arising from a marriage of first cousins, but Helen brushed these aside. The couple were married at Boxted Parish Church on 27 November 1900. Githa's elder sister left to live with her husband at

Croglin and assumed the duties of a Rector's wife with enthusiasm. Sadly, time proved the concerns of the family justified. Helen and Reginald's first child, their son Reginald Hugh, born in 1901, was small in stature and had a deformed foot. Their daughter Ephrata Dorothy, born in 1904, had mental health problems and did not develop normally in adolescence. Helen and Reginald were told that the physical condition from which Dorothy suffered could be treated but her parents decided against it, stating that Dorothy was so plain that having treatment to make her body more like that of other adult women would make no difference. What Dorothy felt about this decision, if indeed she ever knew about it, is not known.

Early in April 1901, Githa and her father travelled to Roundill Farm, Cumberland, to talk to her brother Lawrence about his plans for the future. Lawrence, who was about to marry his fiancée Lucy, a vicar's daughter from Cheshire, now announced his plans to emigrate. John George still cherished the hope that his only son would return to the glassworks. If he had done so, it could have made a great difference to the family's income. But Lawrence's mind was made up. Lawrence wanted a life on his own ranch in the Canadian wilderness and no amount of persuading was going to stop him from emigrating when he felt the time was right. Lawrence and Lucy Clarke were married on 16 April 1901 at St Mary's Church, Rustherne. As they began their married life the couple continued to see their long-term future as lying in the new territories opening up in Canada. The rest of the family thought Lawrence very selfish to plan to drag Lucy away from civilisation but Lucy made it clear she would be happy to go. She was an adventurous woman, she loved the countryside and she loved Lawrence.

The couple eventually emigrated with their two young sons, Eric and Tom, in early 1912. Lawrence obtained a land grant to settle near Wasa in British Columbia. There he set up as a rancher and lived happily with his family in a handsome timber house he built with his own hands. Apart from one visit lasting several weeks to England around 1929, for the rest of his life Lawrence made sure that the Atlantic Ocean remained between him and glassmaking.

That the first two of John George's children should marry spouses connected so closely with the church is interesting, since religion had played very little part in the upbringing of Githa and her siblings. Grandfather John Sowerby, like his father George, had served as a church warden. Regular church attendance on Sundays was an essential part of a respectable life and the powerful Sowerbys would be seen in their local church. But Githa's close relations had previously had no time for the "God-thing", as it was known in the family, and as Githa grew up, religious observance had increasingly been limited to weddings, funerals and christenings. Helen and Lawrence's return to fuller church membership, however, did not tempt Githa to follow their example. She had no religious beliefs and maintained this stance throughout her long life.

Despite his reduced expenses now that two of his children had left home, John George's financial improvidence caught up with him. In 1903, unknown to his wife and children, he was once again declared bankrupt. He could no longer afford to live at Boxted House. After a brief stay in Reigate, he moved his family to an attractive, but much smaller, old house in the historic village of Sutton Courtenay. Positioned on a beautiful site on the banks of the Thames, south of Abingdon in Oxfordshire, Sutton Courtenay lay in prime landscape painting country and John George was happy. Although her loyal cook moved with them, Githa's mother's establishment was now reduced to one live-in domestic servant.

The need for her parents to reduce their expenditure presented Githa's chance of independence and she took it. She had previously been working as an author in a small way and had had a number of poems published in magazines. When the rest of the family moved from Boxted, she and her younger sister Millicent left home for London.

CHAPTER FOUR

Independence

Githa and her sister Millicent set up home in a small London flat and embarked on a full-time career producing children's books. Githa was the leader in the partnership, being a much stronger character than her sister, but Millicent was a talented artist. As a young woman living on Tyneside, she had attended some art classes with John George's blessing, but the distance she had to travel had made attendance in inclement weather difficult and at times impossible, so consequently she was largely self-taught.

Curtis Brown became their agents and the Sowerby sisters' first effort, *The Wise Book,* was published by JM Dent in 1906. It was an immediate success and was quickly followed in 1907 by *Childhood* and *The Bumbletoes,* both of which were published by Chatto & Windus. While *The Bumbletoes* was a fairy story for children and sold very well, *The Wise Book* and *Childhood* were books of verses about children aimed at the adults who read the poems to their offspring. This shrewd portfolio of styles worked extremely well, winning significant sales abroad as well as at home.

In 1906 Githa's youngest sister, Ruth, eased her parents' financial situation further by becoming the third of John George's children to marry someone connected with the church. In November 1906 Ruth married the Reverend Herbert Sawyer at the Parish Church in Sutton Courtenay and went to live in Oxford. Around this time Githa and Millicent took into their household their sister Marjory, who had been left with a paralysed arm following an attack of polio. Thus Githa and Millicent assumed part of the traditional role of the father in the Victorian family – they were the ones earning the money and paying for the care of their disabled sister.

Githa loved Marjory dearly and had no regrets about taking on responsibility for her care. Githa's sense of duty and family loyalty was very strong and if members of the family needed support, then she would always be the one to provide it when her father could not. However she did feel some resentment that, after all the money her father had had through his hands since the death of her grandfather in 1879, and her grandmother in 1896, he seemed unable to support his family properly. John George, it appears, had no qualms whatsoever about expecting Githa and Millicent to become financially responsible for their sister, despite the fact that outsiders would have seen this – and his choice to work as a full-time artist – as extraordinary behaviour precipitating great loss of social status to his family. But just as he had ignored

Githa's misery when he insisted she should help impress guests during his days as glassworks manager, John George was perfectly happy to rely on her financial assistance to enable him to live the life he had always wanted.

The traditional Victorian parent-child attitudes remained in place despite the shift as to who was providing the income. John George required Githa as a matter of course to put his needs before her own. He perceived no conflict between this and his failure to fulfil the male responsibilities that were traditionally used to justify the self-sacrifice of women in Victorian and Edwardian society. A reading of the plays she would later write suggests that Githa was well aware of the inconsistencies in her father's attitude to his role. Her resentment of the situation fuelled a major theme in her work about the necessity for women to become economically independent of men if equality of the sexes was to be achieved.

Once settled in London, Githa took advantage of her new independence to set about putting right the deficiencies in her education. She began attending lectures on social and economic issues sponsored by the Fabian Society. While three of her siblings elected to put conventional religious faith in place of the relentlessly materialistic philosophy of life that had ruled the Sowerbys of earlier generations, Githa chose a different set of beliefs as the framework for her life. She embraced socialism. Finding the Fabian philosophy broadly in tune with her own, in 1905 she decided to join the Society – even though at that time it had no commitment whatsoever to the cause of women's economic independence which meant so much to her.

Anyone wishing to become a member of the Fabian Society was required to sign an application form to say that they had attended two meetings as a visitor and that they accepted the statement of the Fabian Society's beliefs, known as 'The Basis'. The Basis was worded as follows:

> The Fabian Society consists of Socialists. It therefore aims at the reorganisation of Society by the emancipation of Land and Industrial Capital from individual and class ownership, and the vesting of them in the community for the general benefit. In this way only can the natural and acquired advantages of the country be equitably shared by the whole people.

> The Society accordingly works for the extinction of private property in Land and of the consequent individual appropriation in the form of Rent of the price paid for permission to use the earth, as well as for the advantages of superior soils and sites.

The Society further works for the transfer to the community of the administration of such industrial Capital as can conveniently be managed socially. For owing to the monopoly of the means of production in the past, industrial inventions and the transformation of surplus income into Capital have mainly enriched the proprietary class, the worker being now dependent on that class for leave to earn a living.

If these measures be carried out without compensation (though not without such relief to expropriated individuals as may seem fit to the community), Rent and Interest will be added to the reward of labour, the idle class now living on the labour of others will necessarily disappear, and practical equality of opportunity will be maintained by the spontaneous action of economic forces with much less interference with personal liberty than the present system entails.

For the attainment of these ends the Fabian Society looks to the spread of Socialist opinions, and the social and political changes consequent thereon. It seeks to promote these by the general dissemination of knowledge as to the relation between the individual and Society in its economic, ethical and political aspects.[29]

The Fabian Society considered membership of their group to be a privilege and each new candidate had to be proposed and seconded by existing members. Sadly, however, because the membership records in the archives of the Fabian Society are incomplete, it is not now known who proposed and seconded Githa. The evidence today for her joining the Fabians in 1905 seems to depend on word-of-mouth alone. It is also not known how long she remained a member of the Society.

The Fabian Society rules described its work as follows:

1. Meetings for the discussion of questions concerned with Socialism.
2. Meetings of a more public character, for the promulgation of Socialist Opinions.
3. The further investigation of economic problems, and the collection of facts contributing to their elucidation.
4. The publication of pamphlets containing information on social questions, or arguments relating to Socialism.
5. The promotion of Socialist lectures and debates in other Societies.
6. The representation of the Society by public conferences on discussion on social questions.
7. The organisation of conferences of Social reformers, with a view to common action." [30]

Though Githa used attendance at Fabian Society meetings and lectures to fill in some of the gaps in her education, her brand of Socialism was not a carbon copy of Fabian Society policies. Despite the presence among the Fabian Society's ranks of outspoken supporters of female emancipation like George Bernard Shaw, the Society's political agenda was largely a male one when Githa joined it in 1905. The Society had stated in 1884 in Manifesto Tract No. 2 that it considered that "men no longer need special political privilege to protect them against women". However, the Fabians had published no specific document on female emancipation following the failure of one of their committees in 1894 to produce a document the Society felt able to publish, and this failure to act became increasingly unacceptable to its female members.[31]

In 1908 women members of the Society lost patience and forced the hand of the Executive Committee. HG Wells had proposed a motion to insert three new clauses in The Basis, one of which committed the Society to supporting equal citizenship for men and women, but the Executive Committee was opposed to the motion because of the vague way all three clauses were phrased. The women members made it clear that they would vote for the motion unless the Executive Committee proposed an amendment adding to the Basis a commitment to "a reconstruction of the social organisation by enforcing equal citizenship of men and women".[32] It is sad that such tactics should ever have become necessary in a Society dedicated to political and social reform. However, in 1908 the commitment to women's emancipation was finally made, and gradually thereafter the female Fabians became more active and influential within the Society. Whether Githa played any active part in this rebellion by the women members of the Fabian Society is not known.

The 1911 book *My Birthday* [33], written and published six years after she joined the Fabian Society, contains a poem in which Githa makes one of her clearest statements rejecting the system of laissez-faire political beliefs under which she had been brought up. That poem is *Tuesday's Child*.

Each morning as the clock strikes ten
The Wise Man came with book and pen.
"Your Majesty must learn," he said,
"How laws and prisoners are made.
Who is your friend and who is not,
And how much money you have got.
How some are high and some are low,
And how it always must be so."

The lesson over for the day
He shut his book and went away.
Then children came with shining wings
And taught her many other things.
They took her hand and led her down
Into the hot and dusty town,
Where children had no time to play
And people worked the livelong day
To guard and keep her safe from ill
There in her palace on the hill.[i]
And that is how she learnt to be
The wisest Queen in Arcady.

Earning their living still remained of the highest important to Githa and her sister Millicent. They published children's books at an increasing rate. In 1908 they produced *Yesterday's Children*[34]. As a child, Githa had been frightened by stories from *Grimms' Fairy Tales* so she thought of an alternative version that she was sure would keep children interested without scaring them. In 1909, Githa's version of *Grimms' Fairy Tales* appeared with all the horror of stories such as *Bluebeard* left out; but it did not sell well. She and Millicent also produced *The Happy Book*[35] in 1909. In 1910 Hodder & Stoughton published a trio of their books, *Little Plays for Little People, Little Stories for Little People,* and *Little Songs for Little People;* and in 1911 the sisters published *The Merry Book* and *My Birthday*[36] with a different publisher, Humphrey Milford.

Githa was branching out as a writer. Sometime around 1908, she and Millicent met Francesco Paolo Tosti (1846-1916). Singing-master to the children of Queen Victoria, Tosti was a popular singer and song-writer with many friends among the aristocracy and in London's artistic and literary circles. In that year Githa began writing English lyrics for a number of Tosti's love songs and the partnership continued for the next four years.

In 1911 Githa also completed *Rutherford & Son*. Her first adult play went into rehearsal at the Royal Court Theatre at the end of that year. (She had previously published six short plays for children in her 1910 book, *Little Plays for Little People.*) It was a productive year for Githa. She also wrote a one-act comedy, *Before Breakfast,* a send-up of armchair socialists. A curtain-raiser to a MacDonald Hastings play at The Playhouse from 2 May 1912, it ran for 63 performances. And of course, 1912 brought the life-changing success of *Rutherford & Son*.

---

i It doesn't seem too great a leap to suggest that the "palace on the hill" represents Ravenshill, the house where Githa was born.

Journalists were not the only people to struggle to reconcile the beautiful London society woman they interviewed with the dramatist who had created the ground-breaking *Rutherford & Son*. Her family, too, had to adjust their perceptions of Githa and learn to accept her as the person they now knew her to be. Before the triumph of her play, she and Millicent had been thought to be people of no particular social consequence in class-conscious early 20th century London. Now, as the dazzling new woman playwright, Githa was a London lion, with a flurry of articles about her appearing in fashionable society publications such as *The Queen, The Lady's Newspaper, Throne & Country*, and *Nash's Magazine*.

Her sudden change of fortune was not universally popular within the Sowerby family. Githa's elder sister Helen and youngest sister Ruth had enjoyed their superior social status as married women over their three single sisters.[ii] Now their having married impecunious clergymen did not hold quite the sparkle it formerly had. Githa's fame also came as a rude shock to the Sowerbys' rich relations the MacLeans. Sir Francis MacLean, husband of her aunt Martha, previously Member of Parliament for the constituency of Woodstock, had risen to become Lord Chief Justice of Bengal. When Githa's father severed his connection with Sowerby's Ellison Glass Works and chose to re-invent himself as an improvident landscape painter, Sir Francis and Lady MacLean ensured they had as little social contact as possible with their now very much poorer relations. But after *Rutherford & Son*, they decided to add their niece's name to their guest-list at 17 Rutland Gate, Kensington.

To their chagrin the MacLeans found their invitations declined. Githa made it quite clear that she neither wanted nor needed their patronage, though she remained on good terms with their daughter, Violet. She continued to mix with the friends she had previously met through her membership of the Fabian Society and she made many new ones in theatrical and artistic circles.

Just as they were getting accustomed to Githa featuring regularly in newspaper headlines as the sensational new dramatist, she lobbed a fresh grenade in the direction of her shell-shocked family. According to family legend, Githa had seen a photograph in a newspaper of a handsome poet and playwright she had never met. His features so attracted her that she was said to have commented at the time to her cousin Gwen, "If that man ever asked me to marry him, I'd say Yes!" In the flush of her new-found fame she met the man, Captain John Kaye Kendall, and they fell for one another.

---

ii Margaret Helen Sowerby was married to the Revd. Reginald Southwell Graham Green in 1900 and Rachel Ruth Sowerby to the Revd. Herbert Sawyer in 1906.

At 43, Captain John Kaye Kendall was seven years her senior. A writer of light verse and a playwright, he was introduced to Githa at a party at the Messel residence in Stafford Place, Kensington. At the time he had been close friends with another woman, but from the moment he met Githa he had eyes only for her. That evening he accompanied her to the theatre. During the next few weeks John and Githa saw a great deal of each other and exchanged many letters. On 24 April 1912, just three weeks after their introduction, Githa announced that she would be marrying the handsome retired Army officer early in July. Few of their friends had suspected a whirlwind romance and there was great surprise at the engagement.

Captain Kendall came from an old and distinguished Cornish family. He had been invalided out of army service in the Royal Regiment of Artillery in India in late 1903 and was finally discharged on health grounds on 16 April the following year. His father, a Clerk in Holy Orders who had been for some years Professor of Mathematics at the University of Toronto, had returned to England in 1860 to fill a succession of posts as curate and vicar in the Church of England.[37] Once he was grown up, John Kaye Kendall had as little to do with his natural family as possible, preserving links only with two of his brothers. He thought it monstrous that his clergyman father had expected his mother to bear 13 children in 16 years and saw him as a pontificating hypocrite. John's prolonged absences from home, first at boarding school and then in the army, had helped him maintain this distance when he was younger, and he did nothing to heal the breach when he returned to England. Despite this, John seems to have been fond of his mother, dedicating his first volume of poetry to her.

After his boarding school education and military training at Woolwich Barracks, Githa's future husband obtained a commission as 2nd Lieutenant in the Royal Regiment of Artillery on 27 July 1888. He was promoted to Lieutenant on 27 July 1891, and attained the rank of Captain on 17 February 1899. He served 16 years with the British Army in India and Malta before incipient deafness caused by his duties as a gunnery officer led to his discharge.[38] During his final tour of army service in India, John published two small volumes of light verse which were read and enjoyed by the British community in Bombay. After he left the army, several of these poems were collected and re-published in 1905 under the title *Rhymes of the East and Re-Collected Verses*.[39]

Once back in England, John Kaye Kendall quickly became prominent in literary and artistic circles, writing regular poetry for the magazine *Punch* under the pseudonym Dum-Dum. He also had some success as a playwright with the plays *Mrs Bill*, *Dad* and *Laughter in Court*, all of which had brief runs in the West End. Strongly individualistic, he was often asked why he did not write serious poetry. His invariable response to this was a sharp "Why the hell should I?"

It was surely a supreme irony that Githa, an independent woman with advanced ideas who earned her own living, should be marrying a man who wrote amusing verse for a satirical Establishment magazine like *Punch*. *Punch* never lost an opportunity to ridicule, in cartoon and article, the so-called New Woman, whose determination to win economic independence from men the magazine found ridiculous. Perhaps the fact that John was so different from her other friends was part of the attraction for Githa. Maybe she needed a man she could argue with. Certainly she had never before met anyone quite like John Kaye Kendall.

Though it was hard for them to be apart when they had met one another for the first time so very recently, Githa had a script to finish. Her new play, *A Man and Some Women*, was barely started, and Curtis Brown wanted her to get the script to them as soon as possible so that the momentum from the success of her first play was not lost. Though there was no hope of finishing it before her wedding, she took herself off to stay with friends at Sutton Courtenay for a fortnight to work on the play.

As she began work, Githa was filled with optimism. The last time she had sat with pencil and notebook in a boat on the Thames at Sutton Courtenay the outcome had been *Rutherford & Son*. Now, sitting once more in a boat on the Thames, *A Man and Some Women* began to take shape. This time, Githa decided, she would tell a story contrasting greedy, selfish women who depended on men for their support, with a woman who earned her own living and related to men as equals. And she would add a sub-plot that questioned society's stigmatisation of innocent children because of misdemeanours committed by their parents. Githa did as much work on *A Man and Some Women* as she could but time ran out long before she could finish the first draft. After two weeks at Sutton Courtenay it was time to return to London to concentrate on preparations for the wedding.

Having introduced her fiancé to her relatives in the London area, in mid-June Githa took John to meet her parents at the beautiful Georgian Orde House in Whitchurch, the latest home to which John George had moved to continue his artistic career. For all his self-absorption and his thoughtless exploitation of her abilities, there is no doubt that John George was genuinely proud of Githa. It is likely that it was he who in 1912 commissioned the artist George Percy Jacomb-Hood to paint a portrait of her at the height of her fame. In the portrait, Githa is not wearing her wedding ring, so it must have been painted before her marriage in July 1912. Commissioning a portrait is exactly the kind of gesture that John George would have made to celebrate Githa's triumph. He was a familiar figure in the art world in London and would have known precisely the best portrait painter to approach. The cost of such a commission would not have deterred him, despite his perilous financial position.

It was not a visit Githa had been looking forward to and the meeting was not a success. Afterwards John made no secret of his dislike of his future father-in-law. He considered John George's treatment of Githa in the past to have been grossly insensitive and neglectful of her abilities, and he condemned John George's abdication of financial responsibility for his disabled daughter Marjory. Categorising him as a ne'er-do-well, John coined for his future father-in-law a nickname that he took from Lewis Carroll's *Hunting of the Snark*. This was 'The Great Boojum', a particularly lethal kind of snark that lived on a distant shore and had the power to make people vanish. From that time on, in public and in private, John never referred to Githa's father as anything other than 'The Great Boojum', though he did so out of earshot whenever his father-in-law came to visit.

On 8 July 1912, amid great secrecy because they wanted to avoid the journalists, Captain John Kaye Kendall and Katherine Githa Sowerby were married at Christ Church, Chelsea, in the presence of a small number of friends and family. They had known one another just three months. As Githa destroyed all her personal letters and photographs shortly before she died in 1970, the only photograph of her wedding that survives is a newspaper cutting showing the couple leaving the church as quickly as possible after the ceremony. Despite all their efforts to protect their privacy, they had been spotted by a reporter from the *Daily Mirror*.

It might be thought that, as the 43-year-old son of a clergyman who had been to boarding school and then served as an officer in the British army in India, John would have been a person stunted by regimentation and imprisoned by convention. But stuffed shirt he emphatically was not. John did not glide into Githa's life so much as explode into it. With a short fuse and liking nothing better than to say something outrageous to see how many people he could shock at one time, John was larger than life. Only his genial manner and ready sense of humour saved him from being thought rude and insensitive. He was very popular at the Garrick Club where he spent a good deal of time each week with his friends from *Punch* magazine.

There were marked differences between their political views but one thing that John and Githa were agreed on was that they did not want a family.

Having been brought up as one of 13, John had had quite enough of children and did not want any of his own. Though Githa liked children – other people's – and got on very well with them, she was uncertain of how she would cope with children of her own. Githa did not know what loving mothers did, she did not find it easy to show affection, and she was afraid of the responsibility of motherhood. Her career was another consideration, for the life of a successful dramatist was opening out before her. Githa knew from her professional experience as a children's author, that success meant sitting down to write morning after morning whether she felt inspired or not. Life as a professional dramatist would demand the same level of commitment, this time combined with the responsibilities of a wife. And John and she both relished the active social life they were leading. Children would inevitably interfere with this. It was a joint decision. There was no room in their lives for a child. The way ahead would definitely not include babies.

Millicent and Marjory moved into a flat of their own (Githa continued to contribute to the rent) and John and Githa rented a flat at 41 St George's Court, off the Gloucester Road. Their daily routine as professional authors was soon established. Githa sat down to write each morning from 9am, while John sat down in his study to type his contributions to *Punch*. In the evenings they entertained and socialised as much as their still limited income allowed. Githa's playwright's instincts were nourished by being an observer in London at the heart of the country's political and literary life. Though they had many interests in common – theatre, poetry, books, art, classical music – in personality John and Githa were complete opposites. Githa was as quiet, poised and self-contained as John was loud and rumbustious. But their conflicts were creative. They understood each other. And they were happy.

Throughout 1912 Githa's agents Curtis Brown were besieged with requests from abroad for the rights to translate *Rutherford & Son* into other languages. By the end of the year agreements had been entered into to allow its translation into French, German, Dutch, Bohemian (Czech), Italian, Russian and Swedish. The productions that followed, however, had mixed success. In Germany the actors could not cope with the pronunciation of the name "Rutherford". Permission was granted for the play to be re-titled *Romford & Son* for the Munich production but worsening relations with Germany did not help the play's reception in that country. Rights were granted for productions in Canada, Australia and America, and licences were also issued for a number of productions in regional repertory theatres in various parts of England including Annie Horniman's Gaiety Theatre in Manchester and the Liverpool Playhouse.

John was proud of Githa's success and, with his literary contacts, was in an excellent position to help her career, although – true to form – he was not always diplomatic in the way he went about providing such help. Not long after they had announced their engagement, John had written to Githa to say that in his opinion her agents were not handling her one-act comedy *Before Breakfast* as well as they might. This caused Githa to write to Curtis Brown on 16 May 1912 as follows:

Dear Mr Brown

Many thanks for your letters of May 14th and 15th and for your cheque for £31 3s. 8d.

With reference to the amateur rights of "Before Breakfast" it has come to my knowledge that French applied to you for the rights and were told that they were already disposed of to Williams. I cannot understand why their terms were not enquired into, compared with those offered by Williams, and the offer submitted to me. I should much prefer French to have the rights as they are obviously the people to whom everyone applies for a piece of this kind. I understand that French's manager was going to see the piece but was put off doing so by what you said. I shall be glad to hear from you on the matter. I have corrected the proof of the description of "Rutherford" which Williams proposes to send out and return it to you.

I note what you say about the Dutch rights. It seems to me to be very important to get a sum down in these foreign contracts – not from the point of view of the possible value of the play but simply as a guarantee that the adapter will take some trouble to push it – and will not hang it up for a year or more, spoil any other chance I might have, and then throw it over. Hemmings paid £25 for the Scandinavian rights so it is not without precedent!

Yours sincerely
Githa Sowerby

Following some tense exchanges in writing and a meeting with Curtis Brown representatives, the misunderstandings were cleared up and the company remained as her agents with Githa's full confidence. The amateur rights for *Before Breakfast* were indeed assigned to Samuel French & Co, where they still remain. Cyril Hogg, owner of Samuel French & Co, became a close friend of John and Githa, and handled the performance rights for Githa's plays personally until his death.

The fuss about the rights for *Before Breakfast* was to no avail. No companies – amateur or professional – subsequently showed any interest whatsoever in it. The market had changed. There was no further call for plays to be used as curtain-raisers, and repeated attempts by Curtis Brown to sell this wickedly funny exposé of armchair socialists as a musical hall sketch were unsuccessful.

Not long before *Rutherford & Son* ceased its London run, John decided he would like to obtain a professional and objective assessment of the merits of his wife's play. Without saying anything about it to Githa, he approached a contact in the Lord Chamberlain's Office to ask for an opinion.

Charles Hallam Elton Brookfield was an actor and playwright. A member of a family well known in artistic circles, his appointment in 1911, at the age of 76, to the Lord Chamberlain's Office as an Examiner of Plays had caused a storm of controversy among dramatists already angered by the capricious decisions of the censor, and especially the refusal of a licence for Harley Granville Barker's play, *Waste*. The Dramatists' Club, of which John Kaye Kendall was a member, had taken a vote on a motion condemning the appointment, but the result had been so close that no definite action resulted. As John Kaye Kendall subsequently chose to ask Brookfield for an opinion on the merits of *Rutherford & Son*, he had presumably voted against the motion condemning Brookfield's appointment.

On headed notepaper from the Lord Chamberlain's Office, St James' Palace, but marked 'Private and Unofficial', Brookfield replied to Kendall's enquiry on 15 July 1912.

My dear Kendall

My wife and I went to "Rutherford & Son" on Friday. It is a hateful, ruthless, <u>most immoral</u> play! But brilliant and brimful of cleverness. Miss Sowerby has a marvellous sense of character, which is a very rare gift among dramatists – few of them have any at all. I don't know which creation is the subtlest; perhaps "John Jnr" pleased me the most on the whole, though Mr Breon was hardly equal to the part. "Martin" was terribly true (I know his counterpart, a Somersetshire "hauler"). I wonder if the unsparing depiction of all his hateful weakness and vices was conscious cynicism on Miss Sowerby's part or merely unconscious accuracy? He is the typical liberal labourer of today – the <u>actual</u> British working man – educated a little above his station, just enough to muddle his unconvolved (sic) rabbit brain; egotistical, easily gulled, sensual, mean, untrustworthy, disloyal, dishonest, dastardly – yet finally believing himself all the time to be the noblest work of God.

"Mrs Henderson" is a very ingenious study, quite distinct from many superficially similar stage characters: the way she shifted her ground from servility and pleading to unbridled vituperation (rounding even on "Richard" – who, by the way, was not very skilfully defined by Mr Randall) was remarkable and quite original and led up to the climax in a most natural manner.

Of course "old Rutherford" is a masterly conception, but McKinnel – accomplished actor as he is – invests every part he plays so completely with his own personality that the author is rather swamped by the actor – this estimable "suppressed force" would be still more precious if he were a little more assertive in the scenes where he meant to let himself go. After all a theatre is not a back drawing-room, though the modern players seem to think it is.

I liked Edith Olive better in her early discontented scenes than in her more emotional moments: but I can't think of anyone who would have better played the part. Miss Norman might have done more with her chances (or somebody else might have) but she wasn't half bad: I thought her best in her stronger scenes and not quite equal to the "character" touches. Old Agnes Thomas was adequate and dull.[i]

<u>All</u> the characters were <u>real</u> and not stage characters, such as they are in most plays. When I call the piece "immoral" I allude to the reward of selfishness at the end: the hard-hearted old ruffian who has broken the spirit of all his children and turned them adrift is left to a peaceful old age with a willing daughter-in-law and her baby, who bears his name, to solace his declining years. I am afraid I belong to the small remainder of the play-going <u>vieille garde</u> who like virtue-rewarded, vice-punished, happy-ending plays.

Pray forgive me for writing so frankly – you asked me to send me your opinion. I am full of admiration for your wife's brilliant gifts: I hope soon to see them shining forth in a play that shall be pleasant as it is sure to be craftsmanlike and wittily written. Pray don't show her this letter if you think it will annoy her. I don't want her to dislike me.

I hope you are having a very delightful honied (sic) holiday.

Charles HE Brookfield

---

i Edith Olive played the tyrant's daughter, Janet Rutherford, in the first production; Thyrza Norman played the pivotal role of the working class daughter-in-law, Mary, and Agnes Thomas played the nagging, old-fashioned Aunt Ann.

What John felt about these reactionary comments, or the recommendation that Githa should next write a "pleasant" play, is not known; nor do we know what Githa thought of Brookfield's response to her husband's request for his opinion. However, she kept Brookfield's letter among her files of business correspondence, where it was found 96 years later.

Brookfield's letter strikes the only discordant note among the reviews of Githa's play. Unlike the enthusiastic audiences for *Rutherford & Son*, Brookfield was looking for predictability – happy endings with virtue rewarded and evil punished, as in the Victorian melodramas for which he clearly had great affection. And he (like Githa's agents Curtis Brown, who now saw the market as needing her to write something more light-hearted than her first play) seemed to favour the kinds of drawing-room comedy that in the 1950s Terence Rattigan would cite as keeping his stereotyped theatregoer "Aunt Edna" happy. But despite calling *Rutherford & Son* immoral, even Brookfield acknowledged Githa's brilliant gifts at characterisation.

Undoubtedly part of the popularity of *Rutherford & Son* arose because it was the right play at the right time, both theatrically and historically. Ibsen's plays *A Doll's House* and *Hedda Gabler* had raised controversial questions about the role of women in society but they were nonetheless still stories presented from a male perspective. *Rutherford & Son* triumphantly reflected the female perspective, depicting the ruthless domination of his family by an industrialist for whom his glassworks company is before all.

Githa was not the first 20th century woman playwright to enjoy West End success with a play showing life from a female perspective. Cicely Hamilton's second play, *Diana of Dobson's*, had run for 143 performances at suffragist Lena Ashwell's Kingsway Theatre in 1908. It was revived for a further month the following year and toured the country throughout 1909.[40] Like *Rutherford & Son* "By KG Sowerby", Cicely Hamilton's first play (a curtain raiser) had originally been advertised as "By C Hamilton" in an attempt to keep the sex of the playwright a secret until after theatre critics had made their views known. (It should be noted that the only two critics to discover beforehand that "C Hamilton" was "Cicely Hamilton" were also the only two to write negative reviews.) The comedy *Diana of Dobson's*, however, was publicised under her full name.

In 1908 the Women Writers' Suffrage League and the Actresses' Franchise League, of both of which Cicely Hamilton was a founder member, had joined forces to support the campaign for universal women's suffrage with propaganda, plays, sketches and performances.[41] But there is no evidence that Githa was a member of either of these organisations or that she was involved in any way with either the non-militant National Women's Suffrage League (begun in 1897 by Millicent Fawcett), the direct action Women's Social and Political Union (founded in 1903 by Emmeline Pankhurst and her daughters), or indeed any other feminist campaign group. The agenda of the Women Writers' Suffrage League and the Actresses' Franchise League did not include challenging as issues in their own right the suffocating male domination of British theatre or the overwhelming influence of male theatre critics. The Women Writers' Suffrage League and the Actresses' Franchise League were set up simply to help the cause of votes for women. Githa came by an entirely different route to depict women's issues through drama. She campaigned alone, and solely through her plays.

Despite her belief that society must change, when asked by journalists whether she wanted to teach people through her plays Githa firmly denied that she wanted to teach people anything. "Teaching people" was what she remembered suffering at the hands of uninspiring governesses. "Education" was something she believed to be far wider. Education could be many things, including telling people stories that first made them *feel*, and then made them *think*. Education could be *Rutherford & Son* where, in the end, the tyrannical father of the family meets his match in his gentle daughter-in-law Mary, who proves that a woman can be quite as ruthless in fighting for her baby son's future as John Rutherford had been in sacrificing his family to his business.

As luck would have it, *Rutherford & Son* appeared at a time of simmering political activity in England. Change was in the air. The year 1912 would later be tagged by historians as "The Great Unrest". Between 1910 and 1914, membership of trade unions quadrupled and there were numerous strikes. In parallel, the increasingly militant campaign by the suffragettes to gain votes for women was at its height. But the women's movement, which had been diversifying and gaining momentum throughout the 19th and early 20th centuries was not and never had been solely concerned with electoral reform. Its campaigners wanted recognition for women as equals in intellectual ability, family life, sexual relationships, and the upbringing of children. They wanted equal access to education and employment. They wanted equality before the law and in property ownership. Only then would they know respect as human beings in their own right, rather than being regarded as second-class citizens fit only to fulfil roles subordinate to men.

"The Guv'nor's like that with us all – it's always been so," says young John Rutherford of his tyrannical father in Githa's play. "He doesn't like women – never notices them."[42] The word 'suffrage' may not appear anywhere in the script of *Rutherford & Son* but the devastation wreaked in his family by the behaviour of John Rutherford struck a chord with women already becoming politicised in increasing numbers. On 20 July 1912 the Women's Freedom League newspaper *The Vote* openly hailed the work as being "in the truest, strongest sense, a suffrage play".

> "I do not profess to understand the playwright's inmost thoughts, but I do understand what it is that her glowing art depicts. Straight from the heart of life she picks the truth and we stand aghast as she reveals it... Fear, hate, deceit, the fruits of subjection and coercion – how long will men and women be blind to the source of these fertile streams of degeneracy, and to the need for our race of a freer and more vigorous motherhood?"[43]

Though she had never promoted *Rutherford & Son* as a suffrage play, Githa was happy that the women's movement had – unlike the mainstream reviewers – spotted *Rutherford & Son*'s political agenda. She must therefore have hoped that suffragists might also spot the political agenda in *A Man and Some Women*, based as it was on destruction of the myth that keeping women dependent on men produced happy homes full of women who were self-sacrificing, spiritual and pure. She certainly could not count on London's male theatre critics to realise that *A Man and Some Women* was a political play. Githa knew that they would interpret her play as a family drama, just they had with *Rutherford & Son*.

As early as February 1912, Norman McKinnel, the actor who had created the part of the tyrannical father to considerable acclaim, had begun to put together plans to take the production of *Rutherford & Son* to America. After much work and juggling of actors' commitments, all but two of the original cast set sail for New York in October. The play opened in December 1912 at New York's Little Theatre, and ran successfully there for 63 performances. *Rutherford & Son* was well received by the New York audiences, though not with the unbridled enthusiasm that had characterised its run in London. The unacceptable face of capitalism as depicted in *Rutherford & Son* was perhaps a less palatable message for the booming commercial centre of New York than for English audiences during 'The Great Unrest'. The male American theatre critics displayed the same patronising attitudes to women dramatists as their London counterparts, penning headlines such as 'WHEN LOVELY ENGLISH MISS TURNS TO PLAYWRITING.'[44]

Githa had the opportunity to accompany the cast to New York but she decided to remain in London. Her reasons are not recorded but throughout the remainder of her life she bitterly regretted that decision. No doubt she would have enjoyed one or two encounters with the sexist New York theatre critics.

1912, the most momentous year in Githa's life so far, was drawing to a close. She was now 36 years old. She had found a man to marry who had as strong opinions as she had – if very different opinions. John was not the easiest person in the world to live with but he loved and respected her, and with him she could debate issues as an equal. She was now fully accepted as part of London society and she relished London life. And she had achieved extraordinary success as a playwright with her very first full-length play. Although the issues she continued to depict in her plays sprang directly from her life experiences on Tyneside, Githa wrote no more plays that reflected so openly her northern roots. She may not have realised the significance of this at the time but, in writing *Rutherford & Son*, she had finally left Tyneside behind her.

Never again would Githa refer to herself as a children's author. After *Rutherford & Son*, children's books were relegated in her mind to the status of pot-boilers, though she continued to work hard on them and to take great care over their composition. Children's books became for her the routine writing that she needed to do to provide for herself and Marjory, and to help Millicent with her career as an illustrator. Githa was determined never to be financially dependent on her husband, but equally her children's books would never again be the main focus of her creative energy. Her perception of herself had changed fundamentally. She had become a professional dramatist and she would never again describe herself as anything else.

CHAPTER FIVE

A Playwright at War

After the upheavals of 1912 with Githa's marriage and the launch of her play-writing career, 1913 dawned full of hope. Because of the success of *Before Breakfast* and *Rutherford & Son*, several theatres were interested in *A Man and Some Women* and were keen to consider the script as soon as it was available. However, the final version of *A Man and Some Women* was not finished and sent to Curtis Brown until December 1913. Githa and Millicent only managed to publish two children's books in 1912, both re-prints. These were *Poems of Childhood*[45], which was essentially a repeat of their 1908 book *Childhood*, and *Little Plays for School and Home*[46], which was a re-print of their 1910 book *Little Plays for Little People*. They produced no new children's books together at all in 1913.

As early as April 1912, Arthur Bourchier, manager of the Garrick Theatre, had asked that Githa's new play be offered to him if it had not been promised to anyone else, but Githa wanted time to consider which theatre would serve as the best platform for *A Man and Some Women*. She was too well known now for theatres to be able to hide the fact that her new play had been written by a woman. Githa wanted her play to be offered to a theatre manager who would understand its political dimensions and respect its female perspective on the world. American theatre managers too were harrying Curtis Brown for copies of Githa's next play. However, she was advised to secure *A Man and Some Women* a London run before it crossed the Atlantic, as this would enable her agents to negotiate a better deal.

When Curtis Brown wrote to Githa in late 1913 acknowledging the script of *A Man and Some Women* they said they were deeply impressed with it. However, it seems unlikely that they really shared her complete commitment to *A Man and Some Women*. Contrary to their advice that her next play should be something more light-hearted, Githa had not written a comedy, nor was her second play significantly more light-hearted than *Rutherford & Son*.

Githa had ignored her agents' advice because her commitment was to writing from the heart about issues that mattered to her as a modern woman. She wanted to make audiences think as well as to entertain them. She was not interested in writing smooth words for a shallow audience who would leave the theatre as untouched by real issues as they were when they came in. Githa wanted to write about real people; flawed human beings that audiences would recognise as being like themselves or people they knew. She wanted her audiences to leave the theatre angry and sad about injustice and keen that the future should be made better than the past.

Unlike more narrowly-focussed feminists who considered that injustice was the lot only of women, Githa saw that men were just as trapped within stereotyped roles as women. *Rutherford & Son* showed domestic tyranny over his family by the man at its head, but in *A Man and Some Women* the persecutors are female. Their victim is a man who has swapped dominance by his mother and a mistress for persecution by his cold and demanding wife and his two unmarried sisters. The plot of *A Man and Some Women* makes it clear that Githa wanted justice for both sexes, not simply for women.

Although Curtis Brown appreciated what Githa was trying to achieve with *A Man and Some Women,* they were uneasily conscious that much of the momentum from the success of *Rutherford & Son* had been lost with the passage of time since her last play. With Githa fending off journalists in 1912, rather than cultivating her contacts, publicising *A Man and Some Women* in a positive way when it went into production would be that much more difficult, even once a theatre had been found to present it. This time the prejudice against women playwrights could not be avoided; "Miss Sowerby" was too well known.

Harley Granville Barker was the obvious first choice to approach with the script of *A Man and Some Women.* He was a fellow member of the Fabians; an innovator, who was keen to capture the spirit of plays rather than building productions around the use of star actors. His artistic standards were high and he was no slave to fashion. However, despite his past successes, Granville Barker was becoming increasingly disillusioned with the British theatre. First his hopes for the establishment of a National Theatre had come to nothing, then the Censor banned his play, *Waste.* He and his then wife, actress Lillah McCarthy, had recently leased the Kingsway Theatre from Lena Ashwell. Their plan was to put on programmes of classics and new plays in repertory, but the financial risks were proving hard to manage and Barker sustained losses from putting art before commercial viability.

Githa approached Granville Barker informally about her play and, despite his pessimistic mood, he asked to see the script. Her hope was that Barker would accept *A Man and Some Women* for production at the Kingsway but he rejected it. The manner of his rejection was particularly disappointing. It took the form of a letter dated 14 January 1914.

My dear Miss Sowerby

This play is good I do think, but not nearly as good as it ought to be.

In the first place, that expedition is quite obviously put there purely for your own convenience! If you mean that you think that the man and the girl ought to walk off together, by all means let them do it. And then it suffers because black is so black and white is so white. The really dramatic problem, I think, in the matter is when the husband is really subject to spiritual and moral and even physical temptations. I mean when he is torn between a rather fine and dangerous course and one which is the easier and more respectable: when he is drawn back to his home – as nearly every man is – by recollections of happiness and past kindnesses, and by feeling a little bit that probably he has been to blame too, etc etc.

In fact you are rather hard on the wife and it makes her become a wooden figure. But much of it is so excellent. If women really will go on writing about women in this entirely truthful and ruthless fashion, we shall have something like a drama soon.

Forgive this outspoken-ness. It interests me enough for me to wish not to be merely polite.

Very sincerely yours,
H Granville Barker

Granville Barker had only once staged a full-length suffrage play[47] and his pessimism about the future of British theatre was well known, but Githa must have hoped that his concern to be true to the spirit of the plays he put on would have led him to empathise with her political purpose in writing *A Man and Some Women*. She could not fail to find Barker's analysis deeply disappointing. Despite his reputation as a theatrical innovator who had famously thrown off the stilted traditions that had imprisoned performances of Shakespeare for decades, he had interpreted *A Man and Some Women* as a simple love story. Like Brookfield in his comments on Githa's first play, her fellow-Fabian Barker was also looking for certainty at the end of the play: either the hero Richard Shannon must head off into the sunset with Jessica, the modern woman he had fallen in love with, or alternatively, he should return to make the best of it with his persecuting wife. But either of these endings would have destroyed the play's message, for Githa ends *A Man and Some Women* with Jessica demonstrating her love for Richard by letting him go, encouraging him to be free to grow up away from female domination – an ending echoing the departure of Nora at the end of Ibsen's *A Doll's House*.

Granville Barker's comment that the expedition to Brazil had been put there for the playwright's convenience must have been particularly galling to Githa, for in this case she had drawn on real experiences within her own family. Her cousin, Murray Levick, son of her aunt Jeannie, who had joined the navy as a qualified surgeon in 1902, had been seconded to Scott's 1910 expedition to the Antarctic. After being stranded as part of the six-strong Northern Party on Inexpressible Island for the whole of the Antarctic winter of 1911-12, Murray and his companions walked 230 miles across the ice-bound continent to re-join their main party at Base Camp despite being near starvation. He and his group, unlike Scott's own party who all died, survived largely because of Murray Levick's indomitable spirit and his skill as a doctor.[48] And Murray Levick was not the only adventurous cousin among Githa's relatives. Dennis Sowerby, son of her grandfather John's younger brother George (1822-1872), had settled in British East Africa (present-day Kenya) and eventually died there in mysterious circumstances in 1913, and her uncle Charles and brother Lawrence had both emigrated to North America. Why, therefore, should it be considered implausible for her hero, Richard Shannon, to consider going out as scientific adviser on an expedition to Brazil?

Githa might have been comforted had she known that she was in good company in having her work rejected by Granville Barker. He had also turned down the last three plays submitted to him by John Galsworthy and the most recent offering from John Masefield. But she was not aware of this and her response was anger and disappointment. After a couple of poor seasons at the Garrick Theatre, Arthur Bourchier was no longer in a position to consider her new play. *A Man and Some Women* was offered more widely but the response from other theatres was equally disappointing. Eventually only one theatre manager – a woman – accepted the play: Annie Horniman put *A Man and Some Women* into her weekly repertory programme at The Gaiety Theatre Manchester in October 1914.

Githa was forced to face the fact that the mood in the country had completely changed. *A Man and Some Women* was no longer in tune with the times. War had been declared in August 1914. The suffragettes, who in 1913 would have been excited and supportive of another play about women's issues by Githa Sowerby, had suspended their Votes for Women campaign for the duration of the war. They were now fully occupied helping the country by filling the jobs vacated by the men who had enlisted in their thousands to fight. *A Man and Some Women* was not going to get a run in London – at least, not till after the war.

The war, in those early days, was expected to last only a few months. After thinking it over, Githa turned down an offer from an American company to tour the play throughout the US because *A Man and Some Women* had not yet had its London run. She did not bargain for the war lasting for five long years – at the end of which time there was no American offer to resurrect. *A Man and Some Women* was destined never to be performed again until 1996, when it was revived by director Sheila Hannon for the Bristol production company Show of Strength. It has never been published.

When war was declared in August 1914 John Kaye Kendall immediately rejoined the Army. He was seconded to MI5 and sent to serve in Ireland. His service records have not yet been released by the MoD, and we have, at the time of writing, no details of his war-time service. But by the end of hostilities he had been promoted to the rank of Major. Githa missed her husband very much and worried a great deal about the danger he was in. When he returned home on leave he was unable to talk about the work he was doing, which increased her anxiety.

On 6 December 1914, Githa's father died suddenly at Wye Gate in Monmouthshire, the latest home to which he had moved with his wife. Because the death was unexpected, an inquest was held on 14 December. The coroner ruled that John George Sowerby had died of natural causes (angina). Ironically, his obituary in the Tyneside press made much of John George's former prowess as an amateur oarsman, hardly mentioning his connection to the Sowerby's Ellison Glass Works; there was no reference at all to his subsequent career as an artist.

John George is known in the Sowerby family as the person who "went through three fortunes". His will, proved in 1915, revealed the full impact of his refusal to modify his way of life and his frequent moves around the country. Githa's father had spent all he had inherited from his parents and the income his wife brought from her father. His Sowerby's Ellison Glass Works shares, of course, had been sold in 1896, but towards the end of his life he had also gradually sold off the shares he held in other companies in order to maintain his lifestyle. At his death John George Sowerby's estate amounted to just £79. He left his wife, Amy Margaret, in great hardship.

There can be no doubt that John George knew before he died just how precarious his finances had become. Somehow – it is not clear how – despite his bankruptcy, he had managed to continue his comfortable lifestyle up until his death without telling anyone else. He presumably did so in the happy certainty that he could count on Githa to take care of her mother (and perhaps him too, since he could not have anticipated his own premature death). She had after all supported Marjory for years. In the absence of Lawrence in Canada, it seems that John George disregarded his next child

Helen completely and placed Githa in the position normally filled by the eldest child in a family. Was John George aware of Githa's resentment of the role in which he had placed her? Probably not. But John Kaye Kendall knew or he would not have coined the nickname 'The Great Boojum' for John George.

John George's achievements as designer and colour-mixer at Sowerby's Ellison Glass Works produced some fine pieces of art glass and stained glass and as a landscape painter he created several attractive pictures which remain to enrich people's lives today.[49] In his later life he achieved what he wanted to achieve and felt fulfilled as an artist. Neither his wife Amy Margaret, nor Githa and Millicent as his daughters and fellow artists, were consulted about the sacrifices John George expected them to make for the sake of his art. John George kept his financial problems secret. If he thought at all about the ethics of the situation, he clearly concluded that it was only right that his wife and daughters should be willing to ensure he could live and work as he wished. And no doubt his wife Amy Margaret, being ignorant of their true financial situation, continued to expect him to provide her with something approaching the standard of living she had always known. It is perhaps fitting that the less desirable attributes of John George Sowerby should have ended up on the stage reflected in the character of Eustace Gayden in Githa's play *The Stepmother*. However, it was to John George that Githa owed her early exposure to political thinkers with very different views from those traditionally held by the Sowerby family. And because of her father she learnt enough about the glassworks business and the history of her family to write her play *Rutherford & Son*, weaving from her family history her morality play of domestic tyranny, class distinction and the unacceptable face of capitalism.

John George was dead, Lawrence had emigrated and Helen and Ruth were married to impecunious clergymen; Marjory was disabled and unable to work; once more it was left to Githa and Millicent to avert a family crisis. They helped their mother move to rooms in a boarding-house in Broadstairs with Marjory for company. For "icily regular, splendidly null"[50] Amy Margaret Sowerby, who had been born into a wealthy Newcastle family and had lived a prosperous married life, the reduction in her circumstances after her husband's death was devastating. Though she had never previously liked Githa, she now leaned on her most capable daughter for support, and it was Githa who tried to arrange for a little more income to be made available to her mother.

As part of her investigation into her father's financial affairs, Githa wrote to her aunt Bella to ask why there was no income for her mother from shares in Sowerby's Ellison Glass Works. Bella's reply revealed that John George had made over his shares outside the Sowerby family to Uncle Edmund – her mother's brother, Edmund Hewison. She also informed her niece that John George had sold his uncle a considerable number of shares in other companies which might otherwise have produced an income.

Githa was extremely angry at this further evidence of her father's financial irresponsibility. She thought it disgraceful that he had kept his parlous financial situation secret right up to his death, but there was nothing she or anyone else could do. She and Millicent began to work furiously on the production of their children's books. In 1915 they brought out four – *Cinderella, The Gay Book* and *The Pretty Book* published by Henry Frowde, and *The Dainty Book,* produced by Humphrey Milford. All four sold well.

In May 1915 their sister Marjory married Frank Harding, an ex-Army officer, and moved to a house just down the road from her mother's lodgings in Broadstairs. At last it was no longer necessary for Githa and Millicent to contribute to Marjory's care on top of that of their mother. But Githa did not like or trust Frank Harding, who had acquired a reputation within the family for over-familiar behaviour towards his nieces. As far as she could, she maintained close contact with Marjory to make sure she remained well and happy, as well as keeping an eye on her mother. She visited as often as she could.

Meanwhile, the First World War dragged on. As a member of the Fabian Society, Githa subscribed to the belief that wars were precipitated by capitalists for the sole purpose of making money. (Given that the roots of the conflict lay in disputes between colonial powers over territories and markets, this argument had some strength.) However, in 1915, as the flood of wounded soldiers sent back from the front began to overwhelm the hospitals, moved by the humanitarian crisis, Githa tried to give what practical help she could.

Githa, like many of her friends in London's theatrical circles, became heavily involved as a volunteer in the work of the Surgical Supplies Depot in Kensington. The Kensington Depot (afterwards known as the War Supplies Depot) was set up to respond to the sudden and acute shortages of medical supplies and equipment. Like similar organisations that sprang up all around the country, it was a charitable organisation. With Princess Louise, Duchess of Argyll, sixth daughter of Queen Victoria, as its patron, the Depot started out as a small affair based in Phillimore Gardens, Kensington. As the war progressed, it hugely expanded its operations, occupying rooms made available in eight houses in Kensington Square Gardens. The charity was dedicated to the voluntary production of surgical appliances for the war wounded, but it also provided equipment for children's clinics, hospitals, and people who could not afford to purchase the equipment they needed. They also offered a service to surgeons and others who invented new appliances, to have them made and adjusted at the Depot's workshops at cost price or, in appropriate cases, for nothing. Eventually the Depot supplied many thousands of items each week to more than three hundred British and Allied hospitals.

Most of the people involved in making the appliances gave their time free, as Githa did, and the charity attracted many supporters. The French, Italian and Japanese Ambassadors, and the Mayor of Kensington all signed up as patrons despite the fact that the government of the day disapproved of these volunteer efforts, fearing the implication that official care being provided to the war wounded was inadequate. Eventually the Depot would employ more than a thousand volunteers working in shifts.

The Kensington Depot provided a lively social network. It was during her work at Kensington Square that Githa made two significant friends – Isabel May Buzzard (known as May) and Gladys Napier. May, whose husband was serving in France as a Lieutenant Colonel in the Royal Regiment of Artillery, would later have an important influence on Githa and John's lives when the war was over. Gladys Napier (daughter of Sir George White, Governor of the Royal Hospital, Chelsea) and her husband became their lifelong friends.

On 14 July 1916 the *Kensington News* advertised a typical fundraising effort – a grand bazaar. Under the heading 'FOR THE WOUNDED – COME TO OUR PARTY', the War Supplies Depot invited public support to raise money for their production of 45,000 items every week. These items included surgical splints, bandages, swabs, crutches, shrapnel pads, pneumonia jackets, leather stockings, hospital trolleys, dressing-gowns, and bed-tables. Princess Louise was to attend the bazaar to review the Kensington Battalion of the Volunteer Training Corps. Helpers included many celebrities both from high society and the entertainment world – Leslie Henson, Mrs Patrick Campbell, Yvonne Arnaud, Ellen Terry, Vesta Tilley, and Mr and Mrs Gerald du Maurier, among others. The Band of the Welsh Guards were engaged to play and theatrical entertainment was to be offered by George Robey and Alfred Lester, the Strand Theatre Company, and Mrs Jarley's Waxworks. On top of all this, there were sports contests held specifically for the participation of wounded soldiers.

Githa's job as a volunteer at the War Supplies Depot was to sew the leather used in so-called 'stiff boots', which were designed to enable soldiers with foot wounds to walk without crutches. Sewing the leather was hard work, and the pressure to keep up with the orders made the task stressful. In the evenings when she returned home exhausted, Githa would do embroidery to relax. (Her daughter Joan still keeps a framed piece of embroidery her mother did at this time.)

In early May 1917 a journalist from *Punch* visited the War Supplies Depot. *Punch* had been implacable in its condemnation of the evils of war but the writer was moved, in spite of himself, at the sight of what was being done in Kensington Square.

> "Figures talk and here are some very articulate ones. On May 7 orders had come in from sixteen hospitals in England and France for articles the raw cost of which exceeded a thousand pounds, and it was on these that I found the staff at work. All were wanted as quickly as possible and all had to be made by the ladies and gentlemen who have voluntarily given their services to this cause; everyone an amateur and all of them now doing something that but for the War they would probably never have dreamed of... They would, I know, hate to be praised for this willing service; let me say, then, that I am merely recording it. Well, that order of May 7 has long since been completed..." [51]

The order in question was for between 30,000 and 40,000 items and it had been fulfilled in a matter of days. This three-page *Punch* article, first published on 30 May, was repeated the following month in the edition of 27 June, and on both occasions it ended with a plea for donations of money and raw materials.

Somehow, in the midst of her voluntary work, Githa found time to produce another children's book with her sister – *The Bright Book,* published in 1916 by Henry Frowde. She also wrote another play, *Sheila.* The new play highlighted the iniquities of class distinction and explored further the theme of economic independence for women. However, it also examined the very different motives men and women sometimes had for getting married and the serious misunderstandings that could arise as a result.

Sheila fared better with theatre managers than *A Man and Some Women* had done. Its touches of comedy were most welcome in a country wearied by war. Thanks to the support of Sir George Alexander, manager of the theatre, *Sheila* had a run of 19 performances at St James's Theatre from 7 June 1917.

Sheila met with a mixed response from women. Those with more modern views identified with its message but others did not. The writer of a review in *The Ladies' Pictorial* is typical:

> "Of course, Sheila's whole attitude is quite illogical. Why should not a man marry because he wants a son? And what better compliment can he

pay to a woman than to wish that she should be the mother? How many thousands of women make no secret whatever of having married for the hope of children! Are all their husbands to consider themselves insulted? But it is all very charming – clever, witty, tender, womanly…"[52]

When she read this, Githa must have realised, if she had not done so fully before, how deeply ingrained among some women were the old traditional attitudes to marriage that women in her own family had suffered from in earlier generations. The author of the *Ladies Pictorial* piece still assumes their readers would consider it quite normal to approach the choice of a marriage partner as one might the breeding of pedigree cattle. There was still a long way to go before all women saw equality as their right.

Unlike *Rutherford & Son*, which had hit the headlines during the political turmoil of 1912, the suffragettes were completely silent on the subject of the issues raised by *Sheila*. This may have been because the Women's Social and Political Union had been split over what policy to pursue during the war, and in 1917 could no longer speak with a united voice. Or it may have been that, having suspended their campaign for the vote for the duration of the war, in return for the release from prison of all suffragettes in August 1914, they felt duty bound not to stir debate on women's issues while war was still raging.

As might have been anticipated, the play was not particularly well received by the male critics. They considered the story flimsy – "the motive for the… misunderstanding is too feminine or too far-fetched for a mere man."[53] The prejudice of critics against works by women playwrights was by no means ready to be given the last rites. Githa was a realist. But that did not make her disappointment at the limited success of *Sheila* any easier to bear. *Sheila* has never been performed since its brief run at St James's Theatre in 1917, nor has it ever been published.

John returned home on leave from Ireland in time to console Githa when *Sheila* ceased its brief run at St James's Theatre but he could do little to lift Githa's mood. She had begun to feel that no one valued her work as a dramatist and it hurt. Her disappointment revived damaging childhood memories of her inability to please her mother, whatever she did.

Githa was now 41. She and John had both assumed there was no danger of her becoming pregnant. They were wrong. Not long after John returned to Ireland, Githa found that she was going to have a child. This was a shock and certainly not what either of them had wanted. However, they realised at once that they must put aside the decision they had made six years earlier to remain childless and make sensible plans for a new future that included caring for a baby.

CHAPTER SIX

The Playwright at Home

Githa and John gave up their London flat and rented a house called Little Chewton in Sunningdale, as they felt this would be a healthier environment in which to raise a child. It was a pretty house with a veranda and a garden, and stood near the church in the old part of Sunningdale. The house move and her pregnancy forced Githa to give up her voluntary work at the War Supplies Depot. She very much missed the friends she had made there. The baby was due in May and Githa began to try to adjust to life away from her beloved London. She made enquiries among friends and eventually secured the services of a suitable live-in nurse to help when the baby was born.

When Githa was five months pregnant, tragedy struck her sister, Helen. On 9 February 1918, Helen and Reginald's son, Hugh, was found dead in a field adjoining their home at Wetherall, the parish at which her husband was now Rector. Hugh had died instantly from a gunshot wound. He was just 16. The inquest on 16 February was held in the rectory with Reginald's curate as the foreman of the jury. The coroner's jury was told that Hugh, who was home for a few days' holiday from his job as a farm pupil at Newton Regny, had gone out at about 5.30pm on 9 February to check on a rabbit trap he had set earlier in the day. Unknown to his parents, he had taken his father's double-barrelled shotgun with him. The jury concluded that Hugh had slipped on mud while attempting to climb through a wire fence into a neighbouring field and that, having neglected to un-cock the gun, it had caught on something and fired, hitting him in the eye and killing him instantly.[54]

After deliberating for only a short time, the jury returned a verdict of Accidental Death and extended their sympathy to Helen and Reginald. Privately, however, questions continued to be asked both within the Sowerby family and locally about what may really have happened. It was pointed out that an inquest held in the rectory and chaired by Reginald's curate would hardly have been impartial, nor would it have pursued the truth with determination. And why would such pains have been taken to control the outcome of the hearing if there was nothing to hide? By his father's admission, Hugh had been shooting for six months. Hugh would certainly have been taught to hold a gun un-cocked unless he was going to fire it immediately. He would have known that he should not climb through a fence with a cocked gun and that he should at all times hold guns pointing away from him as he walked. In Cumberland in February it would have been pitch dark at 5.30pm, so in any case taking the gun with him had been both dangerous and unnecessary, for what could Hugh be shooting at in the dark with a double-barrelled shotgun? Along with many others, Githa believed that Hugh had committed suicide and that his suicide had been hushed up because of his parents' position in the local community.

The effect of the tragedy on the relationship between Helen and Reginald was devastating. While they kept up appearances in public in their roles as Rector and Rector's wife, in private they barely spoke to one another. At times when communication between them in their home became absolutely necessary, questions and answers were relayed through their daughter Dorothy. And that situation persisted until Reginald's death in 1952.

Hugh's funeral took place in Wetherall the weekend after the inquest and was attended by many members of the local clergy. Githa was unable to undertake the long journey because of her pregnancy and she did not see Helen until some considerable time after the tragedy. Githa and Helen had never been close and it is not known whether Helen confided in her sister at that time about events surrounding Hugh's death or the subsequent problems in her marriage.

On 23 May 1918, Githa gave birth to a lively and healthy baby daughter. She and John named her Githa Joan Peard – the 'Peard' after John's mother's maiden name – but Joan quickly acquired the nicknames 'Bunnie' and 'Jan'. And Githa, with the help at first of the nurse and then a live-in nanny, began life as a working mother – a role she had never wanted and which she felt inadequate to fulfil.

Githa was not what would nowadays probably be called a touchy-feely person, and neither was John. They had both been brought up under regimes that emphasised the importance of self-control and discouraged outward displays of emotion. While John had the British soldier's stiff upper lip, he did show irritation when annoyed and he laughed if he was amused. In contrast, much of Githa's life was inward in its focus and her demeanour was always quiet and controlled. The bleakness of her childhood and the demands placed on her to entertain guests and fulfil a semi-adult role while still a child had turned her in on herself. She had become a bystander, an observer of people; a thinker. She was never demonstrative, even with people she loved, and she kept her feelings to herself.

Though Githa's political views were modern, her code of personal conduct was essentially Victorian and she now measured the manners of those she met against the exacting standards by which she herself had been brought up. She and John would never have dreamed of embracing in public. During their early years together, they once went to stay with friends who lived in a relatively small house. Githa had been shocked to discover that her husband would not have access to a dressing-room and therefore would be forced to dress and undress in the same room with her.

Apart from the disruption of the First World War, Githa's life with John had, in general, followed the path they had planned together. But then Githa Joan Peard Kendall arrived. At least John was at home on leave from Ireland when the baby was born (while Githa was in labour he took refuge in the garden and furiously mowed the lawn), but he was still attached to MI5 for the duration of the war and Githa soon had to learn to adjust to life as a working mother without him around to befriend her, give her confidence, and make her laugh.

Someone who was by nature less self-contained than Githa might have found the adjustment to life as a mother easier. Like most people in her social position at that time she had engaged a live-in nurse to do all the less enjoyable parts of baby care, but because of this Githa had fewer opportunities to become relaxed in her new role. While she felt entirely at ease with other people's children and they loved spending time with her, Githa found herself on edge when with her own child. This was partly because she was determined from the start to instil in Joan the importance of high standards of behaviour, but also because she could not rid herself of the fear that something terrible might happen to Joan and that if it did it would be her fault. Githa instinctively opted for caution in face of anything that might affect Joan's safety and welfare.

Unfortunately, the older Joan got, the more heavily the responsibility of being a mother weighed on Githa, and the more difficult she found it to relax and enjoy her daughter. Her approach to motherhood remained largely rooted in the 19th century and she became extremely restrictive. She would not allow her daughter nearly as much freedom as other girls of her age were given and this had a damaging effect on their relationship. As she grew older, Joan increasingly felt that it was impossible to get close to her mother or to talk to her about anything important.

John finally retired from the army in October 1918, having been promoted to Major, and returned home permanently. He embraced the opportunity at last to get to know Joan properly. Though he had originally set his mind against having children of his own, he took great pride in his baby daughter and as Joan grew she began to resemble her father in temperament more and more. She had the same determination and adventurous spirit, the same lively personality, and the same quick temper. Joan and her father became very close but, given the similarity in their personalities, they also tended to argue a good deal, even at times throwing things at each other. Despite this stormy relationship, her father was the parent to whom Joan would have gone with any problems. She never felt she could confide in her mother.

When Joan was 18 months old, the family moved back to London and the resident nurse was replace by a live-in nanny, Ada Ling. Ada was a farmer's daughter from Norfolk. She was warm, caring and sensible, and Joan thrived under her care. With John and Githa occupied with their busy social and working lives, Nanny was everything to Joan. When Joan went to stay with her various aunts, Nanny went with her. When Joan went on holiday to the seaside, Nanny went with her. When Joan became ill with pneumonia at the age of five and almost died, Nanny nursed her. Nanny remained part of Joan's life until she was 11. Then Ada had to return to Norfolk, following her mother's death, to take care of her father and younger brothers and sisters. Her departure left an aching gap in Joan's life. She missed Ada terribly.

At the age of six, Joan contracted infantile paralysis while staying with aunt Marjory in Broadstairs. Githa's premonition that something terrible might one day happen to her child seemed to be coming true. Githa rushed to her side by the first train she could get and for three weeks Joan drifted in and out of consciousness while her family looked on helplessly. The first sign that Joan might recover occurred when she began to look around her while being wheeled around Broadstairs in a spinal carriage. Joan did eventually come through her illness but she was left with a weakness of the back for which there was no cure.

As a result of her two serious illnesses, Joan was considered too delicate to go to school until she was ten. She had to leave the kindergarten she had been attending prior to her illness, so Githa engaged a governess to teach her at home. Joan was neither a willing nor an attentive student. Over the next few years a succession of governesses followed. One, who was French, gave notice when Joan ran out of a lesson and hid behind a chest on the landing. Another, who played the banjo, lasted an even shorter time after it occurred to Githa that John might have noticed that she was pretty.

The presence in their household throughout Joan's early childhood of a nanny and the governesses enabled John and Githa to continue their professional lives and the full social life they had had prior to the war. On his discharge from the army John had resumed his regular contributions to *Punch* and Githa continued to write children's books with Millicent. In 1918, soon after Joan's birth and before the war ended, she and Millicent completed *The Bonnie Book,* which was published that year by Humphrey Milford. After this first post-war book, they settled down to the routine production of one children's book a year. In 1919 *Childhood* was re-printed for a second time by Chatto & Windus and, in 1920, *The Dainty Book* was published by Humphrey Milford, and JM Dent, Githa and Millicent's first publishers, re-printed *The Wise Book* in 1921.

Despite her busy social life and work commitments as a professional writer, however, Githa was determined not to be as remote from Joan as her own mother had been. Joan spent far more time with her parents than Githa had ever spent with John George and Amy Margaret Sowerby. If John and Githa had no social engagements Joan would go down to the drawing-room every day after tea and spend the evening with her parents. And as Ada had every Sunday afternoon and evening off, Joan had Sunday lunch and tea with her parents every week, and they were usually joined by Millicent. They played card games and board games, and John in particular encouraged Joan to read good books. When she was younger her father read her stories and, as soon as Joan had learned to read for herself, he chose books for her. He insisted she read Dickens, which she dutifully ploughed through but hated. Her introduction to Jane Austen was happier. She needed no encouragement from her father to read and re-read all Jane Austen's novels many times.

Joan was never taken to the theatre as Githa considered such entertainment unsuitable for a young girl. Had it not been for the more modern approach to motherhood of her parents' friend Gladys Napier, with whom she often spent her Saturdays, Joan would hardly ever have visited the cinema until she reached adulthood. Gladys told Githa very firmly that she was being ridiculous and regularly took Joan and her daughter Pat to see all sorts of films regardless of Githa's objections.

John in particular was very fond of animals and he and Githa were happy for Joan to have a pet. Her first dog was a black and tan collie called Mitch that she adored. Mitch went everywhere with her. When he died Joan was given a pet Pekingese by her great-aunt Bella, who bred pugs and Pekingese dogs.

As Joan grew stronger John began to take his daughter out on Saturday mornings for walks, pointing out to her places of interest and telling her stories from history. Then father and daughter would sneak into an ice cream parlour and eat as much ice cream as they could before returning home, where they would get into trouble from Githa because they were too full to eat their lunch properly. Githa never accompanied John and Joan on these trips. She had always hated walking.

Despite Joan's health problems, Githa and John felt that on the whole they had achieved a good balance between their working and social lives on the one hand and their responsibilities as Joan's parents on the other. In 1920, however, while home life continued as usual, tragedy entered John and Githa's social circle. Their close friend May Buzzard, who lived in Kensington Square not far from where the War Supplies Depot was based, was diagnosed with leukaemia. May was dying and she knew it. The circumstances were especially tragic, for May was completely alone. Her parents were both dead; her only brother had emigrated to America in 1903; her husband had been living apart from her in France with another woman ever since the end of the war; and she had no children. May's many friends rallied around her and she became wholly dependent on them for emotional support throughout her long and painful illness. By the time she died in August 1922, aged only 46, May had become particularly close to Githa and to Gladys Napier.

After May's death, a letter arrived addressed to John from a firm of solicitors asking him to make an appointment to visit their offices. On his return from the solicitors Githa asked, "What was all that about?" and John told her the extraordinary news that was to change their lives completely.

When May first learned of her terminal diagnosis two years before she died, she became determined to ensure that her estranged husband did not benefit financially by her death. May was a wealthy woman and in her last will and testament signed on 18 December 1920 (and proved in the High Court two months after her death), she named John Kaye Kendall as one of her three executors. After a large number of separate bequests in cash and kind to her many friends, May left some money and two fine family portraits (one of her grandfather and one of herself aged 17) to her brother in America. She set aside an amount of money to be used for the upkeep of her mother's grave and finally, in an extraordinarily generous gesture to her two closest friends, she left her large house at 18 Kensington Square and her sizeable residual estate to Githa if she wanted it or to Gladys Napier if Githa did not. A clause in the will added that, if the bequest was accepted, it must be understood that 18 Kensington Square should not be sold during the lifetime of whichever of her two friends accepted the bequest. May also directed that, irrespective of what happened to the house, Githa and Gladys should personally see that all her correspondence was destroyed immediately after her death.

The bequest was a huge shock to John and Githa, who had known nothing of May's plans. The Buzzard family were upset when they learned the terms of May's will but they did not contest it. Perhaps they feared the public scandal that would have ensued if it had become more widely known that May's husband had left her for another woman after the war ended and had shown no care of May during her long and painful illness. Or it may have been that May's estranged husband had money in his own right or access to it. His failure to inherit on May's death does not seem to have affected his standard of living. He was married again within weeks, this time to Elizabeth Wrangell Huene, the daughter of Baron Hoyningen Huene. May's erstwhile husband lived comfortably in a fashionable part of France for the remainder of his life, keeping bees and writing articles on natural history.

Though John had his army pension and his earnings as a writer, and Githa had the earnings from her children's books and the royalties from regular productions of *Rutherford & Son* in Britain and abroad, they were not well off. May's estate was valued after tax at just under £44,000. The bequest gave the Kendalls the opportunity to improve their living conditions immeasurably. By moving to a house in such a fashionable area they could give Joan a far better future than they would previously have been able to afford. After thinking it over, Githa decided that she would accept the bequest. It is testament to the fine character of her friend that Gladys Napier never resented Githa's good fortune or became jealous of the affluent way of life that now opened out before Githa and John.

Sadly, however, this was not the case with Githa's sister, Ruth. In 1923, the year in which Githa moved into her prestigious new home, Ruth's husband, the Reverend Herbert Sawyer, died of pneumonia aged only 43. Ruth's 12-year-old daughter Barbara was at boarding school and her mother did not visit her when her father died, nor did she write to her about it. Instead, the news was broken to Barbara by the headmistress. Because their home was a vicarage, her landlord, the Church of England, gave Ruth three months from the date of Herbert's death to leave the house. When Ruth's daughter returned home for the school holidays it was to a different house and her father, whom she had adored, was never spoken of again. Barbara was devastated, but could share her grief with no one. Ruth, who in any case had never been close to Githa, contrasted her own straitened circumstances with her sister's affluence and her grief turned to bitter jealousy. This caused tension between Joan and her cousin Barbara and prevented them from becoming real friends until adulthood, when Barbara was finally able to share with Joan the pain she had suffered when her father died.

18 Kensington Square, Githa's new home, was a house with a distinguished history. Kensington Square is one of the oldest in London, having been laid out originally in 1685. The present day Kensington Square contains some of the most expensive properties in the metropolis, the average price for a house there in 2007 being £5.7 million. The beautiful garden in the centre of the square is reserved for the exclusive use of its residents and right up to the present day those residents have seen to it that the square has been protected

from encroachment from the nearby fashionable shopping area of Kensington High Street.

The house had formerly been the home of John Stuart Mill. May Buzzard's parents bought it on their return from Army service in India. It was attractive and spacious and very different from the flat in which John and Githa had previously lived. The establishment came complete with a live-in staff of four plus two daily domestic helps, all of whom needed to be retained if 18 Kensington Square was to be run in the manner expected of the wealthy families who lived in this most prestigious of London squares.

Once the legal formalities had been completed, Githa, John and Joan moved into their new home. From the start, Githa loved it. Her life had been a financial struggle for more than 20 years since her father had severed his connection with Sowerby's Ellison Glass Works and now Githa no longer needed to worry about money, though she continued to do so from force of habit. She and John could have engaged a housekeeper but Githa decided she could not afford it and that she had no choice but to run the house herself. This was an unwelcome development for it was the role she had dreaded being condemned to ever since she was young, remembering the limited existence within which her mother had been confined at Ravenshill, Hall Garth, Field House, and Chollerton House.

The world of Amy Margaret Sowerby, however, bore little resemblance to the world in which Githa now lived. As Ray Strachey's comprehensive history of the women's movement, *The Cause*[55], shows, life for women by the 1920s was dramatically different from the restricted and intellectually impoverished existence that had been the norm for middle-class women in 1876 when Githa was born. By 1923 many of the causes for which so many women had fought throughout the 19th and early 20th centuries had been won. Girls were routinely given a proper education instead of only being taught 'accomplishments'. Teachers in girls' schools were properly qualified and girls were expected to pass examinations in academic subjects just like boys. The science of obstetrics had made many advances and the use of ether during childbirth had become socially acceptable after its use during the birth of Queen Victoria's fourth and youngest son, Prince Leopold, in 1853. Following the publication in the 1880s of information about birth control, couples were limiting the size of their families and women were no longer slaves of perpetual childbearing. Divorce was available to women[i] (though not

---

i From 1857 a man could obtain a divorce on the ground of his wife's adultery, but a woman faced with her husband's adultery had also to prove him guilty on an additional ground such as cruelty or desertion.

yet on equal terms with men), and mothers could be awarded legal custody of their children. It was no longer lawful for an unaccompanied woman in a public place to be arrested as a prostitute, to be subjected to a forcible medical examination which branded her as a prostitute even if she was not, or to be imprisoned if she refused such an examination. Women could attend university lectures and take degree level examinations, though battles over the formal award of degrees still continued. Women could practise as doctors and lawyers; they could stand in local and national elections; they could become Poor Law Guardians and members of school boards. Women could take cases to law in their own right.

The impact of the First World War, in particular, had brought significant change. The extent of the change is perhaps best summed up in Prime Minister Asquith's moving 1915 tribute in Parliament to war heroine Nurse Edith Cavell after the news was made public that she had been executed by the Germans. "There are thousands of such women," he said, "but a year ago we did not know it."[56] Prior to this, Asquith had been implacable in his opposition to the granting of votes to women, feeling that they were weak beings, incapable of exercising political judgment. During the war years, while the men were away at the front, industrial employers discovered that women workers were enthusiastic, reliable, hard-working and learned new tasks quickly.[ii] Because of promises made to returning servicemen, not all the gains made by women during the war years were retained. Within a year of the ending of hostilities, returning soldiers resumed their jobs and many women were sent back to the home. But vastly more women had experienced full-time employment outside the home in a wider range of occupations than ever before. Many more women now knew that they were able to maintain themselves independently from men if they wished. Not only that, once they did so, they could retain their own savings, and they could own property in their own right. The goal of women's economic independence from men was becoming more achievable, although a woman's average wage remained much lower than their male counterparts which still made independent life very difficult for working women.

Even so, progress was being made. Although women would not achieve equal voting rights until 1928 when women over 21 were given the vote, in 1918 the franchise was extended to include property-owning women aged 30 and over. The final victory of universal suffrage was in sight. It was becoming evident to the majority that there was no logic in denying the vote to 21-year-old women if 21-year-old men were considered mature enough

---

ii They could also of course be employed on lower rates than men because they were unorganised and were generally undemanding about pay levels.

to vote. From the moment the franchise was extended to include property-owning women over 30, political parties were forced to consider women's views and how women might vote if their views did not prevail. With May Buzzard's legacy of 18 Kensington Square, Githa's status in society had been raised by the acquisition of individual political power in her own right. In addition, she now lived in a house in one of the most fashionable squares in London and had the money to afford the lifestyle that went with it. In the newer, freer world of the twenties, Githa was moving in social circles far above that attained previously by members of her family.

Githa quickly found that running the large house at 18 Kensington Square herself was not a good mix with life as a working mother. No longer could she settle down to write from 9am for the rest of the morning. Her 'Do Not Disturb' notice on the door had no effect. She was constantly interrupted by staff wanting her immediate response to such important matters as why the butter had failed to arrive, and her output of children's books slowed to a stop. Had Millicent not had commissions from other writers, this might have crippled her ability to earn her own living as a book illustrator. As the only one of the five Sowerby girls who never married, it was now essential that Millicent should establish a career that was separate from that of her sister. Fortunately the quality of Millicent's illustrations was well known and soon books began to appear where Millicent collaborated with authors such as Rose Fyneman and Natalie Joan instead of Githa. Among other commissions, Millicent also provided illustrations for editions of *Alice in Wonderland* and *A Child's Garden of Verses*, both of which sold well.

Despite no longer working together, Millicent and Githa remained in close contact after the Kendalls moved to Kensington Square in 1923. Githa was relieved to see her sister's success as an independent illustrator. That same year Githa completed another play – *The Stepmother*. She did not have to look far for an issue around which to build her fourth full-length play. Even though the provisions of the Married Women's Property Act had taken effect nearly 40 years before, many husbands still expected their wives to allow them to control their money and made trouble if there was any resistance. The story of *The Stepmother* revolves around the importance of women not giving in blindly to this pressure. It seems likely that Githa's anger over her father's financial irresponsibility and the hardship her mother suffered during her old age as a result, may have influenced her creation of the unlovable Eustace Gayden, the villain of the piece. At all events, Githa gave Eustace no redeeming features whatsoever.

Seven years had elapsed since the production of *Sheila* at the St James's Theatre and it was 12 years since the triumph of *Rutherford & Son* made

Githa Sowerby a household name. Very little 1923/24 correspondence between Githa and Curtis Brown has survived so it is not known whether her agents were involved in marketing the play to London's theatre managers and, if so, which theatre managements were approached.[57] In any event, if Curtis Brown were involved, their efforts were unsuccessful. *The Stepmother* was eventually given its first and only performance by a private club called The Play Actors at the New Theatre on Sunday 13 January 1924.

The Play Actors was a club founded in May 1907 to benefit the position of the working actor and actress[58], through the production of original works by English authors, Shakespearean plays and other classics, along with translations of well-known foreign works. Plays accepted and performed by The Play Actors were given one performance on a Sunday when other theatres were dark. The New Theatre was loaned for the performance of *The Stepmother* by Lady Wyndham (formerly actress Mary Moore) and Sybil Thorndike. The play was produced by Sir George Alexander, son of the late actor-manager Sir George Alexander who had arranged the run of *Sheila* in 1917 at what had then been his St James's Theatre.

The performance of *The Stepmother* was a glittering social occasion. The programme states that Lady Wyndham and actor Colonel Robert Loraine were to receive members and their friends on the stage after the performance. *The Stepmother* received an enthusiastic reception from the audience and Githa appeared on stage to acknowledge the calls of "Author! Author!", though, as she disliked speaking in public, Sir George Alexander replied on her behalf.

The Stepmother was reviewed in a number of papers and magazines during January 1924, accompanied by displays of production photographs, and comment was on the whole favourable. The magazine *Illustrated Sporting and Dramatic* expressed astonishment that "such a play should have to be presented by a play-producing society, instead of by an ordinary management whose fortune it might easily make"[59]. Another reviewer called it "a most interesting piece of work in which the author's handling of character holds the attention as closely as its absorbing theme"[60].

Despite this enthusiasm and the suggestion by a number of the critics that *The Stepmother* should be given a run in London, no theatre management came forward. This time there was no Annie Horniman to mount a production at Manchester's Gaiety Theatre. Her company had collapsed in 1921. The reign of the actor-manager had been replaced by an era of commercial syndicates. Once again the male-dominated British theatre steadfastly ignored the work of a woman playwright. The unpublished script gathered dust on the shelves of Samuel French & Co and *The Stepmother* was not performed again until 2008, when it was produced by a woman director, Jackie Maxwell, at the Shaw Festival Theatre in Ontario, Canada, to some acclaim. The script published by the Shaw Festival to accompany the Canadian production sold more than 800 copies and a further print-run had to be ordered. *The Stepmother* has never been published in Britain, nor has it been professionally performed in this country after that one initial performance by a private club.

Githa had already stopped writing children's books. Although she could draw some comfort from the Lena Ashwell Players' tour of *Rutherford & Son* around London venues in 1923, yet again her hopes for a success in the theatre with a new play had been dashed. Bitterly disappointed, and convinced by the lack of response to *A Man and Some Women, Sheila* and *The Stepmother* that no one was interested in her work any more, in 1924 Githa gave up altogether. She was to write nothing else for publication for the next ten years.

Apart from feeling she no longer had the energy to keep struggling for recognition against the British theatrical establishment, Githa may also have felt that the opportunity to take a sabbatical from writing was too tempting to resist. She had worked as a professional children's author for almost 20 years, as a dramatist for 12, and had been writing poetry long before she began to earn her living as children's author and playwright. But stopping writing would be a great personal loss. Not being a person who talked freely to people other than her husband and a few very close friends, Githa's writing had been the outlet for her inner feelings, her intelligence and her political views. To live without play-writing meant suppressing the on-going development of an essential part of herself – giving up her creativity forced her to become even more inward-looking than before.

Her decision to stop writing plays, in fact, had implications for her whole framework of beliefs. Githa had finally achieved her goal of complete economic independence but she had achieved it partly through wealth she had inherited from a friend. The Fabian Society, which was publicly committed to the nationalisation of land and property, believed that much harm was caused to society by the 'idle classes'. If Githa had not previously left the Society[61], as a new recruit to the idle classes in 1923 she would surely have felt morally obliged to do so. But to stop writing was her decision and she followed it through. Suppressing the outward show of her political views and deliberately masking her high intelligence, Githa began to play the much more limited role of a woman who had been born into the wealthy and fashionable world of 18 Kensington Square. In the end, inevitably, it changed her.

In 1928 when Joan was ten her parents finally felt she was strong enough to attend school and they enrolled her in a small private school off the Gloucester Road. Joan enjoyed attending outside school but would much have preferred to go to boarding school, as the children of many of her parents' friends did. Boarding school, however, was a step too far for her mother. Githa was also unwilling to take the risk of sending her daughter to a finishing school abroad. Instead Joan was sent to an expensive and highly regarded day school called Glendower in the Cromwell Road. Here the work was much harder than she had known before and Joan was even expected to take examinations.

Glendower provided the kind of wide-ranging education for which Githa had longed as a girl but Joan did not take after her mother in that respect. She had always enjoyed English Literature, History and Art, and she loved taking part in school drama productions, but she disliked her other subjects and she dreaded the examinations, some of which she knew she would fail. To avoid this Joan pretended to be ill. Worried, Githa made an appointment for her with the doctor and Joan rushed there early in order to see him before her mother arrived. He asked about her schoolwork and she explained she was likely to fail her exams. The doctor informed Githa that Joan was "outgrowing her strength" and should follow a less demanding timetable, studying only the subjects she liked. Githa was extremely suspicious but felt compelled to accept the doctor's recommendations. John visited Joan's school to tell the headmistress the news and Joan's timetable at Glendower was confined to the study of History and Literature.

After completing her time at Glendower, Joan attended secretarial college where she learned shorthand and typing. Her father made it clear that he would not allow her to seek paid work with her new skills. This was not due to fears for Joan's health. Her father's reasoning was that his daughter should not seek paid employment because she did not need the money and she would be taking the job away from someone who did. Joan did not mind this at all. Once she had completed her secretarial training her parents gave her a small personal allowance. Joan made her formal entrance into London society as a debutante in 1936 alongside her friends from other wealthy families and led a hectic social life. She had a great deal of fun, most of which she made sure her mother did not find out about because she would have put a stop to it if she had. "My mother's attitude made me deceitful," Joan says regretfully.

Around 1929 Githa's brother Lawrence, with his wife Lucy and his sons Eric and Tom, visited England for the first time since the family emigrated in 1912. They stayed for several weeks with Githa and John in London – a far cry from Lawrence's ranch in the wilds of British Columbia. Lawrence found the atmosphere of London so stuffy and confining that the windows of 18 Kensington Square had to be kept open during the whole visit. It was a good thing it was summer and there was no smog. He did, however, make one concession to the more sophisticated life that London offered. He took Joan and his two sons to see Noel Coward's *Bitter Sweet*.

The main reason Lawrence had returned to England was to market the prototype for a humane animal trap he had invented, rather than to see his family, but he took the opportunity to visit his mother for what they both knew would be the last time. After his departure back to Canada, Amy Margaret Sowerby named Lawrence and Githa as joint executors in her will, even though she was well aware that Githa would have to do all the work of administering the estate as Lawrence would not be there. Lawrence, as her first child and her only son, had always been her favourite.

On 13 November 1931 Githa's mother died at her rooms in Broadstairs. Githa was present at her death and took care of all necessary arrangements, as her mother had known she would. Amy Margaret's will was proved at the High Court on 5 January 1932 and her estate after tax was valued at £437 4s. 4d. In accordance with her wishes, the money was divided equally between her children.

Without reference to Githa or her sisters, and with no authority in the will instructing him to do so, the solicitor handling the estate sent the historic Sowerby family photograph album to Lawrence in Canada, leaving Amy Margaret's daughters with almost no tangible record of their family's history. The dark red and gold album had always had pride of place on a table in Amy Margaret's sitting-room and was of great sentimental value. Her children and grandchildren had pored over it, fascinated by the pictures of the family's wealthy past. They could do so no more, and the precious album was later accidentally destroyed in a fire at Lawrence's ranch.

Fortunately for the families involved, however, Lawrence was so distressed by the loss of the album that he spent many hours putting together a large collection of other family photographs, all of which he and Lucy carefully named. The couple were also avid photographers and chronicled their own life in detail following their departure from England. These wonderful photographs and other memorabilia were passed down to Lawrence's son Eric and then to Eric's daughter Joan, and it is these photographs that have been painstakingly restored by Lawrence's great-grand-daughter Shannon. When Shannon emailed more than 200 family photographs to England, her English relatives had their history restored to them after 78 years. The family photographs in this book are just some from this collection.

After her mother's death in 1931, the burdens on Githa were once again eased. In 1934, after her ten-year sabbatical, she suddenly decided to take up writing again. The reason for her decision is not known but at the end of 1934 a new children's play by Githa Sowerby appeared as the Christmas show at Croydon Repertory Theatre. *The Policeman's Whistle* was premiered on Christmas Eve. It ran for two weeks to full houses. It has never been published. Few people are even aware that Githa Sowerby ever wrote a full-length play for young children, let alone one that was professionally produced.

The Policeman's Whistle tells the story of a boy king who is naughty and spoiled, but who is brought to his senses by a policeman with a magic whistle that makes everyone dance. There is a doctor with magic pills that make people's clothes turn into the clothes they deserve, and twin girls of nine who befriend the young king and show him the error of his ways. Despite the fact that Joan was approaching 17 – she would become a debutante the following year – Githa named one of the nine-year-old twins in the play 'Jan' (one of Joan's nicknames in the family). The theatre programme states that the playwright's daughter Joan had "graciously given permission" for her name to be used.

Githa may have returned to writing to find some intellectual activity sufficient to take her mind off the prospect of the boring round of lunches and teas at which all the mothers of debutantes planned the social events that would form part of the season the following year. Or maybe Githa was trying to pretend to herself that Joan was still the child who she could keep safely at home. If she thought the latter, it was a delusion the dangers of which Githa was soon to realise and record in another play.

For many years it was believed that *The Stepmother* was Githa's last work for the theatre but in 2008 the manuscript of a previously completely unknown play by Githa Sowerby, *Direct Action*, was found among her play-scripts and business correspondence. It can be dated to 1937/38 by a mention of a romance between Greta Garbo and Franchot Tone that was hitting the headlines at that time, and a reference in the dialogue to the song *I'm Putting all my Eggs in one Basket*, which featured in Fred Astaire and Ginger Rogers' 1936 film, *Follow The Fleet*.

The implication from the text of *Direct Action* is that it was the Hollywood affair between Greta Garbo and Franchot Tone (the latter still being married to Joan Crawford at the time) that had alerted Githa to the importance of preparing children for the reality of life in the 1930s. However, it seems much more likely that it was the very public extra-marital relationship between Edward VIII and Wallis Simpson that actually triggered the writing of

Direct Action. In 1936, Joan and her fellow debutantes attended Madame Vacari's school for deportment to prepare for their presentation at the palace by learning the niceties of court etiquette and how to curtsey to royalty. For weeks before, through the round of lunches, dinners, dances and glittering balls, the debutantes had been planning their outfits for the day when they would go to Buckingham Palace for the garden party where they would curtsey to the King. But when that day finally came, instead of remaining on the terrace as the whole procession of debutantes passed by and curtseyed to him, Edward VIII left after a while to return to Mrs Simpson in a back room. This caused consternation and deep embarrassment and, though the discourtesy was put right eventually at a low key affair attended by King George VI after his brother's abdication, it was not the same.

For Githa, who had once refused to allow Joan to accompany Gladys Napier and her daughter to a party at the house of actress Athene Seyler, because their hostess was not married to the man she had lived with for years, the King's very public affair with a married woman must have been very shocking. But Joan had now been launched into London society. Githa could no longer shelter her at home. She finally saw the sense of Gladys Napier's warnings against bringing Joan up by the standards of two generations earlier, and she could only hope that Joan, who was now free from parental restrictions, had enough common sense to protect herself.

Typically, although Githa did not feel able to acknowledge to Joan that she had been wrong, she wrote about her new realisation in her last play, *Direct Action*. Unlike Githa's earlier plays where the dramatic conflict is between men and women, the central conflict in *Direct Action* is between two sisters. The character of Elizabeth Ellison, an old-fashioned mother of three children, is contrasted with that of her sister Stella, who has been divorced and lives very much in the modern world. Aunt Stella steps in, taking the 'direct action' of the play's title, to protect her niece and nephew from making serious mistakes through their naive behaviour with members of the opposite sex. Githa gives the misguided mother the surname Ellison, echoing the title of Sowerby's Ellison Glass Works and suggesting that she based the character on herself. *Direct Action* deals with none of the gritty issues that preoccupied Githa in her earlier plays (economic independence for women, domestic tyranny, etc). Unlike her previous works, it does not end with questions. *Direct Action* ends with Elizabeth Ellison reluctantly entering the 20th century following which all the protagonists live 'happily ever after'.

Direct Action has never been performed. Just as the First World War struck the final blow that killed Githa's chances of success with *A Man and Some Women*, so the Second World War did the same for *Direct Action*. By the time the script was finished, war was about to break out. Not long afterwards the theatres closed for the duration of the conflict. If Githa hoped that Joan would get her message of regret by watching this comedy being performed, that hope was doomed to disappointment. Joan did not even know her mother had written *Direct Action* until the discovery of the manuscript in 2008 in a hat-box full of memorabilia.

The approach of war brought an end to the fashionable life in Kensington Square. In 1938, despite the stipulations of May Buzzard's will, John and Githa decided to sell number 18. Perhaps they reasoned that May would have understood their concerns with war against Germany imminent. But in any case, selling made sense. Joan was leading a hectic social life and was hardly ever at home. Githa had grown weary of running such a large house when they no longer needed the space. After a brief stay in a London flat, she and John purchased a much smaller (though still very elegant) house at 4 South Bolton Gardens. Their new home could be run with just a daily domestic help and Githa's devoted cook, Florence Ford, who had been with her for many years.

War was declared shortly after the Kendalls moved to 4 South Bolton Gardens. Githa began to be troubled by a recurring dream that her house had been bombed. John and Githa briefly rented a house in Sidmouth and Joan moved in with friends in London, but the dream of bombs continued. One morning after yet another such dream, Githa got up and told John that he must go up to London to get all their furniture and possessions into storage. John obediently went to London by the first train the following morning, carried out Githa's wishes, and returned to Devon the same day.

Three days later, 4 South Bolton Gardens was bombed and completely destroyed. "My mother was 'fey'," Joan says, for this was not the first time that one of Githa's premonitions had come true. The house was never rebuilt but their furniture was safe and they were able to reclaim it when they moved to Wokingham not long afterwards. Millicent joined them there and they remained in Wokingham for the majority of the war years before returning once more to London.

At the start of the war John had taken Joan along to MI5 headquarters to see if she could be of help in a secretarial capacity, as the service was short of clerical staff. She was immediately taken on as a shorthand-typist and worked alongside other clerical staff in the cells in HM Prison Wormwood Scrubs, where MI5's offices were then situated. The work was extremely interesting and she felt she was contributing to the war effort. Now free of parental supervision, Joan made the most of her freedom, leading an active and enjoyable social life. After dating a number of boyfriends, in 1939 she became engaged to a young lawyer, Ian Smith, whom her parents both liked very much.

Unfortunately, however, Ian's parents disapproved of Githa and John as playwrights and authors. Ian's maternal grandfather had been a highly respected member of the British community in India (he owned Muir Mills) and his parents considered Joan "a fast London girl", who was leading their son astray. The dislike was mutual as Githa did not feel the match was good enough for their daughter. John had an additional objection. He did not want Joan's married name to be something as ordinary as Smith, asking her: "Can't you at least hyphenate it?"

Fortunately, Gladys Napier took a hand, roundly telling Githa how ridiculous her and John's attitude to Ian's parents was and that she should stop being so stuffy. The young people overcame the objections of both sets of parents and later the same year Ian and Joan were married. Within four years Githa had become grandmother to two boys, Michael (born 1941) and Nigel (born 1943), both of whom she adored.

Githa stopped writing again after completing *Direct Action*. This time she would never restart. When the war ended in 1945 she was nearly 70. The world had changed too much for her to feel confident of saying anything that a post-Second World War theatre audience would want or need to hear. It was very sad. It could all have been so different. There were some compensations however. During the next few years Githa's personal life was more fulfilled than it had ever been. No longer responsible for Joan, and having no responsibility either for the upbringing of her grandchildren, Githa could relax. She enjoyed her grandsons' company as she had never felt free to enjoy that of her daughter. She became very close to Michael and Nigel, and they to her.

Githa, however, never lost her Victorian values. John's hearing was rapidly deteriorating and in his frustration his temper became more volatile. If a lamp would not work the moment he switched it on it would go flying across the room followed by an outpouring of swear words. When John's new deaf-aids refused to slip immediately into the right position and cure his hearing problem they suffered the same fate. Githa felt that she had to protect her grandsons from the bad language that their grandfather sometimes let fly during his perpetual battles with inanimate objects. "Your father is the rudest man in London," Githa told Joan, adding that she could not let Michael and Nigel sleep in the small bedroom next to their grandfather's dressing-room any more in case they should overhear what he said. In vain Joan told her mother that Ian sometimes used bad language too.

In 1951 Githa and John bought Coigns, a house in Virginia Water, where they could be nearer to Joan, Ian and the boys. Despite the fact that he was approaching 82, John began to explore the new area with a soldier's thoroughness. His club life had come to an enforced end because he could no longer hear conversations. He no longer had any creative work to do as *Punch* no longer wanted his light verse. He had always done a lot of walking throughout his life but now it became even more important to him. He was still physically extremely fit and each afternoon he would set off to explore the countryside on routes he had planned out beforehand with the use of ordnance survey maps.

On 11 January 1952 John set out on a new route that took him across railway lines in the woods near Egham. The tracks were guarded only by a kissing-gate and he waited at the side for a goods train to pass before crossing to continue along the right-of-way through the woods on the opposite side. The clanking of the wagons on the first train masked the noise of a second train approaching from the opposite direction on the other line. Still watching the rear of the departing first train, John walked straight into the path of the second. It was travelling at 45mph and was only 15 yards away when he stepped on to the track. The driver braked but he had no hope of stopping in time. John Kaye Kendall was killed instantly[62].

When he had not arrived home by 5.30pm, Githa rang her daughter, and Joan and Ian contacted the police. They were told immediately that there had been an accident and Ian was asked to come to the police station. Joan stayed with her mother while Ian had to suffer the wretched experience of identifying his father-in-law's body. There was little Joan and Ian could be thankful for after such a horrific occurrence but at least they were able to break the news to Githa themselves rather than putting her through the ordeal of being told the news by a police officer calling at her house. At least they were able to tell her immediately that John's death had been instantaneous.

At the inquest on 16 January the coroner's jury brought in a verdict of Accidental Death. It was established that even a person with normal hearing would not have been able to detect the second train approaching because of the noise of the first. However, the jury made no recommendations that greater controls over the crossing should be installed or that warning signs should be erected.[63] Following the nightmare of the inquest and the funeral, Githa and her family were left to recover as best they could. After the loss of their vibrantly alive husband, father and grandfather, Coigns seemed very quiet and bereft.

Because of his pride in his Cornish ancestry the family had a plaque erected in John's memory on the wall of St Brevita Church, Lanlivery. Though he was no church-goer, they knew he would have liked that. The affectionate tribute of *Punch* magazine owner EV Knox, included in John's obituary in *The Times* on 16 January 1952 must have been of some comfort:

"Dum-Dum's first contribution to *Punch* was in 1902, and he continued to write until fairly recently, so that his signature became almost institutional, and his craft in giving to his light verse the tolerant, if cynical, outlook of the London clubman was obtained by much reading of poetry, as well as from the true bent of his own mind. There was never a man of more forthright views, expressed so forcibly in private life: but he mitigated them with a personal geniality that prevented alarm. One remark of his about a modern writer will always be treasured by his many friends. 'He could not even write poetry, much less light verse.'

Dum-Dum seemed to look and feel no older at 70 than at 50. For many years he dined regularly once a week with those members of the *Punch* staff who were responsible for the final make-up of the paper, and his sayings became proverbial. He loved Cornwall, from which his family came, and was remarkable for what he described as 'amused affection' for animals, dating perhaps from the mules of his Indian battery, and extended to almost every kind of bird and beast. As a cadet in a contingent from Woolwich that helped to line the streets he had witnessed Queen Victoria's Jubilee procession, and had not, perhaps, found anything more magnificent in our national life thereafter. He was an excellent friend."

Shortly after John's death, Githa made her own will. She made provision for the continuation after her death of a monthly allowance she had been making for some years to Millicent and recorded that the only reason she was making no provision for her faithful cook Florence was that Joan's husband Ian had promised that he and Joan would take care of her. It was a simple will. Githa left everything to Joan, and named her lawyer son-in-law Ian as her executor.

About a year after John's death and much to the relief of her family, Githa decided to leave Coigns and move back to London. London was where all her friends were and where she felt most at home. Joan offered to help her mother to find a suitable flat but, with a characteristic gesture of independence, Githa refused all help and said she would make her own arrangements.

Githa and her cook, Florence, moved to a flat in Lowndes Square soon afterwards but the new flat was not a success. It was on the ground floor and turned out to be located just above a squash court, so Githa was constantly disturbed by people entering and leaving the building. In addition, as Joan expressed it, "My mother was just not a Lowndes Square girl." Joan found her mother another flat in Melbury Court, which Githa liked much better. She lived there for ten years until the lease expired, before moving to her final home, a large and elegant flat at Campbell Court.

On 26 September 1958 Githa's beloved sister Marjory died of cancer. Githa, now aged 82, broke the news to Lawrence in a letter posted on 5 October[64].

My Dear John [Lawrence went by the first name of John after he emigrated]

I was as usual very glad to get your letter. I have had a broken-up sort of time since I got it, being needed at Broadstairs with Marjory – first for a fortnight to give her maid-cum-nurse a much-needed holiday, then home for a week when I was told she was better. Then I was rung up early in the morning to say she was very ill so I packed up and went. She knew me but I could see she couldn't last much longer, and was with her till she died the following afternoon.

I am sorry to give you this news. We all seem to have been so much separated throughout our lives but somehow the ties hold and it is saddening when they break. But if you had been with her as much as I have through her illness this last year you would be glad for her. She wanted to go and had perfect faith in a happy after-life. She stuck to her church and a parson-friend came in to say the prayers for the dying, there was a requiem at 9am in the church the day of the funeral and a lot of friends and flowers at the service. She died on September 26th, so quietly that I did not know it had happened. Barbara [Githa's niece, Barbara Sawyer, a trained nurse] *was there, so kind and such a help.*

I have been feeling very tired and rather the worse for wear but shall be myself again shortly. The drawback to being 82 is that one can't stand up and take it as one expects to do! Or not as well.

I don't think I have any other news. The boys [Githa's grandsons Michael and Nigel] *were in great form these last holidays and are now back at Fettes* [Fettes Academy in Edinburgh]. *They had a bumpy flight from London to Edinburgh and had to hang around for half an hour in a queue before landing.*

Jan [Githa's daughter Joan's family nickname] *has damaged her back, nearly and all-but slipping a disc which you will know is the really smart thing to do now in the medical world. But she is looking wonderful after an enforced rest. She is rather upset at her hair going so grey – too soon at forty I agree but she is still a pretty woman.*

Write soon and let me know how you both are.

Much love
Judy[i]

In 1960, Florence Ford, who had worked for Githa for 30 years and was devoted to all the family, died of cancer. She was very much missed by everyone. Githa was now in her mid-eighties and was not an easy person to look after so finding another live-in helper to take Florence's place proved very difficult. Eventually Joan did find another helper, a Scot called Miss Innes, who fulfilled the role very well, but Githa in her final years had become almost regal in her manner towards those outside her family. She was not in the least appreciative of anything Miss Innes did, described her "someone from the artisan class" and spoke to her very dismissively. After a particularly hard day, Miss Innes said feelingly to Joan, "I hope your mother goes before me because no one else would put up with her!"

Joan herself visited once or twice a week and took Githa out to lunch. Michael and Nigel, now both grown up and working, called whenever they were staying in London overnight. They found these visits rather tiring because Githa wanted to stay up talking every night until the early hours. But her grandsons both loved her very much and kept in close contact. They had a pied-à-terre in Queen's Gate and always made sure that their grandmother had as many visits as possible in spite of their work commitments, taking it in turns to go to see her.

Joan also arranged for a private doctor, Dr McClay, to visit her mother on a monthly basis to check on her health. Apart from being a highly qualified physician, Dr McClay had an air of affluence about him. He did all his visits in a Rolls Royce and invariably dressed in a pin-stripe suit, which Joan felt helped him to match up to her mother's exacting standards. When Dr McClay eventually died, Joan had difficulties finding a suitable replacement. Githa's verdict on her new young Australian doctor was not wholly favourable. She agreed that he was a nice young man but said it was a pity he did not know the proper way of entering and leaving a room.

Towards the end of her life Githa suffered a little from arthritis and had some short-term memory loss, but in general she remained extremely fit. She outlived her second live-in helper, Miss Innes, who died in 1969, and another live-in helper was found who took care of her during the last few months of

---

i Githa sometimes called herself by the nickname Judy but she was not generally known by that name either in the family or outside it.

her life. Githa outlived by many years her Levick cousins. Ruby Bailey (née Levick) died of tuberculosis in 1940, and her sister Gwen, to whom Githa was very close, died of coronary thrombosis in 1956. Githa also outlived her brother and all four of her sisters, Helen having died in 1953, Marjory in 1958, Ruth and Millicent in 1967, and Lawrence in 1968.

Githa was not close to Helen or Ruth, so their passing meant relatively little. She kept in touch with Lawrence by letter right up to his death in a nursing home, but as she had not seen him for 40 years his death also did not have a major impact on her emotionally. However, the death of Marjory saddened her a great deal, and Millicent too, who had worked with Githa for so many years on the production of their children's books. Throughout her life Millicent had visited Githa at least once a week. Her passing in 1967 left a gap in Githa's life that could not be filled. Githa could write speeches full of emotion for the characters in her plays but she had never been any good at talking about her own feelings. She did manage, however, to admit to Joan, "I really miss that irritating little creature." For Githa that was a huge admission. If only she could have cried it would have been some release but Githa had been taught from an early age that crying was weak and cowardly. She could not cry for Millicent, any more than she had been able to cry for her husband.

Githa Sowerby died on 30 June 1970, aged 93. A few months before her death, she destroyed all her letters and photographs, saying that no one would be interested in them. That was certainly not true as far as her family were concerned and not for the first time Joan was deeply hurt at something her mother had unthinkingly done. But as for the public's interest in her, Githa had a point. There was to be no report in the press of the death of Githa Sowerby. *The Times* did not mark her passing with an obituary. It was as though her achievements and fame had never been.

Her family, however, did add a professional as well as a personal tribute to Githa on the commemorative plaque to John Kaye Kendall in St Brevita Church, Lanlivery. The church authorities initially objected to the use of the word 'dramatist', for reasons that they declined to explain (and which no doubt would have defied logic if they had). They eventually gave way under pressure from the family, and the tribute on the church wall is a fitting one:

KATHERINE GITHA, AUTHOR and DRAMATIST

Githa had no religious beliefs but she would have liked the wording of that.

CHAPTER SEVEN

Through the eyes of her daughter

This chapter was written following nearly a dozen visits at roughly six-weekly intervals to Joan Smith, beginning in April 2008. The contents have been approved by her as a true record of her reminiscences of her life with her parents.

The portrait by Jacomb-Hood on the cover of this book hangs on the wall in my living-room and I can see it from the chair I usually sit in. It was painted in early 1912 at the height of Ma's fame over *Rutherford & Son* and it's been part of my life ever since I was born. It's a fine early 20th century likeness of a very beautiful woman and I know I'm very lucky to own such a painting.

But Ma's appearance in the picture isn't at all like my mother as I remember her. She looks so young in the portrait even though she was 35 when it was painted. I think it's probably accurate for the way she looked in 1912 because some of the theatre critics who interviewed her at that time thought Ma was barely out of her teens when she wrote *Rutherford & Son*. But I was born six years later, in 1918, when Ma was 42, and I only have the vaguest recollection of her hair being auburn. She was an older mother and I remember her hair being grey.

When I was born my mother was working as a professional dramatist and children's author and a lot of my initial care was done by a live-in nurse. Then when I was 18 months old I had a nanny who stayed till I was 11. Everyone had nurses and nannies in those days in the social circles my parents moved in, so the quality of childhood you had depended on what sort of a nanny your parents got for you. I was lucky. I had a wonderful nanny called Ada Ling, and I loved her very much. She came from Norfolk. She was born on a farm, and was one of ten children. She used to tell me stories about it.

It would be very easy for me to say that the reason I wasn't very close to Ma was that I was brought up by a nanny and I must admit I've often said that to people myself. I've certainly said it to some theatre directors who have wanted me to share my innermost thoughts about my mother when I've only just met them, and when I didn't know what they intended to do with whatever information I gave them. But the reason I wasn't close to my mother isn't as simple as my having been largely brought up by a nurse, a nanny, and governesses. That was just part of it.

Having a nanny till I was 11 didn't stop me getting close to my father. Pa was the poet John Kaye Kendall. He was so noisy and vital and alive and you always knew exactly what he thought about everything. No one could possibly overlook Pa. He didn't mind what he said to anyone any time – sometimes he was just outrageously rude, really awful – and Pa and I had the most frightful rows. I remember once throwing a hairbrush at him because he'd made me so angry. And another time when we were walking along the road together and had an argument, I snapped, "Well, I didn't ask to be born!" and Pa replied angrily, "Oh yes, you did!" But I loved him very much and if I'd had any problems it would have been Pa I would have gone to and asked for help. I would never have felt able to confide in Ma, because she was about as different from Pa as it is possible for a human being to be.

Looking for Githa is a very apt way to describe how I feel about my mother. I'm 91 but I'm still wondering what sort of a person she really was. I knew who Pa was all right – no one could fail to – but not Ma. You could only see the outside of her. She kept the real person inside hidden, and she was always very controlled and 'proper'. Whenever she looked at me I always felt she was judging me in some way, to see if what I was doing or saying came up to scratch. That was probably what her mother did to her, too.

Ma didn't know how to relax. Though she had a good sense of humour and found comedians like George Robey just as funny as everyone else did, I never remember her letting herself laugh freely. She had this set code of conduct and she stuck to it so closely that her real self was completely hidden under it. She wore it like a cloak. I never even recall seeing Ma with her hair loose or walking around the house in her dressing-gown.

I didn't understand this at all when I was a child but now I think it was because Ma had such an extraordinary life. Her mother didn't like her; neither did her nurse; and because she was clever and had a strong sense of duty her father used her to fulfil responsibilities he should have taken on himself. And her life fell into compartments. First she was wealthy while her father was still at the glass works, then she was poor when her father became an artist, then she was wealthy again because of *Rutherford & Son* and the bequest from May Buzzard. First she was an unknown writer, then she was famous, then people forgot about her. Ma had so many lives she didn't know which one to choose, and I don't think she knew which Githa she really wanted to be.

Pa adored her and for him to have proposed to Ma so soon after he met her was absolutely in character for him. If she'd said no he would have pursued her for ever and a day until she said yes. I wouldn't be surprised if Pa hadn't proposed to Ma the first day he met her. But for Ma to accept his proposal within three weeks of first meeting him was so out of character for her that I've never been able to understand how it happened. She was always so cautious in everything else in her life, but she wasn't in the least cautious about making up her mind that Pa was the man she wanted to marry. She knew she wanted to marry him when she hadn't even met him and had only seen his picture in the paper.

Pa must have solved the riddle of who Ma really was because they were very happy together. Somehow he managed very quickly to get Ma to trust him and to share her innermost thoughts with him. But I don't know how he managed it in three weeks. I tried for 52 years to get close to Ma and I couldn't do it.

Although as a child I spent time with my parents every evening if they weren't going out or having a dinner party, they didn't talk about anything important in front of me because it wasn't thought suitable to talk about things like politics, religion, private family matters or current affairs in front of children. I think Ma retained her socialist beliefs throughout her life though. Most of the time she kept them quiet, probably to avoid unnecessary arguments with Pa, but what she believed comes through in her plays.

Despite this, though, Ma was still an awful snob when it came to who she would allow me to associate with. Ma and Pa always tried to ensure by fair means or foul that my friends were people they considered "suitable", and they would find ways of freezing people out if they didn't approve of them. At first when I wanted to get married they were against it because, even though they liked Ian, they didn't think this was a good enough match for me. Ma and Pa had to give in, though, in the end. Lady Napier pointed out to Ma that Ian's grandfather, Sir Henry Ledgard, had owned Muir Mills, and had been a very important man in India.

After Ma inherited May Buzzard's house and money and we moved in 1923 to 18 Kensington Square, people always seemed to be coming round for Ma to help them out financially and I think Ma found it very difficult to say no. Thyrza Norman often visited and Ma always knew before she arrived that she would ask for money for cigarettes. Thyrza was very poorly off, especially after John H Leigh divorced her and she married a struggling young actor. But if it hadn't been for Thyrza's encouragement Ma would never have finished writing *Rutherford & Son*, and it probably would never have been produced if Thyrza's then husband hadn't put it on at the Royal Court, so I think Ma felt she owed Thyrza something as well as liking her as a friend.

Ma and Aunt Millicent (who was always known as Aunt Mill) were very good needlewomen and, even though Ma had plenty of money from May Buzzard's bequest, she still made a lot of her own dresses and mine too. I think that's why the heroines in two of her plays, *A Man and Some Women* and *The Stepmother,* are fashion designers – it was a business Ma felt she knew something about. Ma could even make evening dresses, though evening dresses in the twenties and thirties were of a simple design – long, slinky and figure-hugging – so they weren't that difficult to make. And Ma and Aunt Mill made beautiful underclothes – Aunt Mill especially. Although my clothes were always nice I would still have much preferred to have had shop-bought things, but being able to make clothes enabled Ma and Aunt Mill to help out our cousins Ruby Bailey and Gwen Levick, and Ruby's daughter, Winifred, with clothes, as the Levicks had so little money.

Ma was keen on my education and she very much wanted me to do well, but of course my education was interrupted when I was a child because I had pneumonia and infantile paralysis and nearly died. I wasn't a very good student and some of my governesses didn't stay long, which must have been very annoying for my parents. After going to a little private school round the corner I changed to a much better school in the Cromwell Road, and there I found the work much harder. We had to wear terrible berets at that school – it was mortifying. I enjoyed Art and Literature and History and I really loved being in school drama productions, but I was no good at Maths. (I was really surprised when I found out that my paternal grandfather had been a Professor of Mathematics. I certainly didn't inherit that talent.) I remember Ma saying once that she was sorry for one of the mothers she knew whose daughter wanted to go to Cambridge. At the time I was really surprised but I was also rather relieved, because I thought Ma meant she was against women going to university, and of course I had no ambitions whatever to go there. Now I realise that Ma might have made that comment because it was *Cambridge* that her friend's daughter wanted to go to – at the time Cambridge accepted women students for lectures and examinations but refused to award degrees to women, and they didn't change that policy until 1948. However, there was still a belief that having had a university education made girls less marriageable so Ma may been referring to that, and been relieved that I didn't want to go to university.

Ma spent a lot of time reading and we had a lot of books in the house. We also belonged to Mudie's Library and we used to get books from there. Ma had the *Morning Post,* the *Telegraph* and *The Times* delivered every day and she occasionally read *Queen* but she didn't have that delivered. I don't know what books Ma read or what plays she saw, though she and Pa must have gone to see the Gilbert & Sullivan comic operas. I was brought up on Gilbert

& Sullivan. My husband was, too. We could go through the whole of *Trial by Jury* word for word when we were having tea.

Ma and Pa never argued when I was around but they must have done when they were on their own because my father had that sort of personality, and Ma used to get furious with him when he was rude to people. When Aunt Mill came to Sunday lunch he would say outrageous things just to wind Ma up and then look innocently across the table at her and say, "Why are you kicking me?" He had such definite views about everything and said exactly what he thought. Ma and Pa weren't demonstrative. It wasn't a lack of feeling – it was a lack of touch. The only surviving picture of their wedding day shows Ma and Pa leaving the church and walking side by side some distance apart. I know they were hurrying to get away from the *Daily Mirror* reporter but they aren't even holding hands. I think people should feel they can relax enough to look happy in public on their wedding day. Ma wasn't allowed to cry as a child so she couldn't even cry when my father was killed. It's so cruel to bring people up to deny their feelings, but that's the way the Victorians were. Tears were thought of as weakness. And because that's what they'd been taught, that's the way Ma and Pa brought me up. I can't cry either. It's very wrong. Tears are given to us as a release and we shouldn't be taught not to use them. But all the Sowerbys were brought up to deny their feelings. Granny Sowerby and all my aunts and great-aunts were the same. Their upbringing crushed all the spontaneity out of them.

My great-aunt Bella, short for Isabella, is easily the relative I remember best from my childhood because we went to stay with her often at her home at Toddington Manor near Winchcombe in Gloucestershire – not far from Cheltenham. Aunt Bella and Uncle Hugh (who I don't remember because he died when I was eight) were very wealthy. Most people in the family liked Aunt Bella but they looked down on Uncle Hugh because he was a ship-owner, came from Belfast, and had come up from nothing. He'd married into the Sowerby family because of his wealth and skill as a businessman and he'd ended up as a majority shareholder and chairman of the board of the Sowerby's Ellison Glass Works. He'd helped the Sowerbys make a lot of money but they all thought Uncle Hugh had no taste and that he'd just bought Toddington Manor to show off. In the family Toddington Manor was known by the nickname of "the Houses of Parliament with jaundice" because of its over-the-top architecture and the ochre-coloured stone. It's owned by Damien Hirst now and he's doing a lot of restoration there. I'm sure he wouldn't have approved of that nickname.

Aunt Bella's great interest in life was breeding and showing dogs, so she liked the Manor because there was plenty of space and she could use the stables as kennels. She bred pugs first of all, and then she changed and bred Pekingese.

Most of the dogs lived in the kennels but she kept some of them in the house as well. Because of that I could never take my dog Mitch with me when we went to stay with Aunt Bella. It was such a shame. Mitch would have loved to run around in the big grounds there and I missed him a lot when he had to be left at home.

Uncle Hugh was apparently a bit of an awkward customer. It's said that he was asked during the First World War if he would lend his Rolls Royce cars to transport injured soldiers and that he refused because the cars had just been re-upholstered and he thought the soldiers might bleed on the seats. Apparently he added that he "didn't want to add to the gay Bohemian life the soldiers were leading". Thank goodness Pa wasn't there when he said it or he'd have just exploded. Pa knew about it, though, and he never forgave Uncle Hugh for having such an awful attitude to the soldiers.

Aunt Bella went stone deaf when she was quite young and she had a big metal ear trumpet. She never struck me as a very happy person and as a child I was quite in awe of her. I always remember her wearing black, but I expect that's because for most of the time I knew her Aunt Bella would have thought of herself as being in mourning. Sometimes I would go to stay with Aunt Bella just with Nanny, and at other times I went with my parents. Now and again there were really big family gatherings there, because Toddington Manor was so large it could accommodate everyone. Aunt Bella and Uncle Hugh hadn't been able to have children, which was very sad for them, so unless some of my other cousins happened to be staying there I had no one to play with. Not that my cousins were good company for me if they did happen to be staying there when I was. The nearest one to me in age was Barbara Sawyer, my Aunt Ruth's daughter, and Barbara was six years older than me, which is a lot when you're a child. As Ma didn't have me until she was in her forties *all* my cousins were older than me, and they all seemed to delight in trying to take me down a peg or two, including Barbara. They thought I was spoilt because Ma was famous. All Ma's sisters were jealous of her fame.

Under other circumstances going away to stay in a big manor house might have been fun, especially one where there were lots of puppies I could help to look after. But when I was a child I found Toddington Manor a really terrifying place to be. It was such a huge building with stone floors and lots of cloisters with suits of armour standing around. It was more like a cathedral or a museum than a house. When I went there with Nanny I wasn't quite so scared because Nanny held my hand when we went up the main stairs and past the stained glass window with its pictures of the devil, and hell, and the people netted up ready to be forked into the flames. But when I went to Toddington Manor with my parents and without Nanny, it was much worse.

I used to have to go down to the drawing-room on my own to say goodnight to them all, and then walk back up to the nursery by myself past that window to go to bed.

That staircase is huge and wide and cold, and the steps are really very big to a small child. I had this feeling that if I made no noise then whatever might be lurking in the shadows might not realise I was there, but whatever I did the soles of my shoes still clattered or scraped and each step echoed loudly all round the hall. Walking up towards that window was like walking into the mouth of hell itself. As a child I could only see the bottom half of the stained glass picture with its green image of the devil and the terrified people who were going to be forked into eternal fire. I couldn't see the top of the window where all the good people were being rewarded and going to heaven. But I might not have found it all that comforting even if I *had* been able to see to the top where all the good people were. I might have found God quite frightening too. He doesn't look all that friendly.

I'm not exaggerating when I say that I had a haunted childhood because of that window. Even in the daytime I would do anything to stay out of the main house. It was fortunate that Aunt Bella bred dogs because I was able to spend all day down at the kennels helping with the puppies and no one thought anything of it. But after dark there was no escape.

As I was never taken to church during my childhood and neither of my parents was religious I don't really know now why I found the picture of hell so frightening. If I hadn't been taught about heaven or hell, why was I so scared I might be caught by the devil and forked into the flames? But I was, and I never told anyone how I felt. Not even Nanny. I knew no one would understand. They would have just told me not to be so silly and that it was only a picture made of pieces of coloured glass. No one ever noticed that I looked scared, though I'm sure I must have done.

In that respect I suppose I was a bit like Ma. She had a very vivid imagination or she wouldn't have been able to write the books and plays that she did. She had been frightened as a child by some of the horrific details in *Grimms' Fairy Tales* and had had nightmares as a result, which is why she published a version with all the horror left out. And when Pa read to me from a book called *Monsters of the Deep* it made me frightened of the sea for years. He never knew.

My great-aunt Nan used to come to Toddington Manor sometimes and I remember her quite well. Aunt Nan was a sweet, gentle lady, but she was quite eccentric in her old age. She used to ring the Harrods order line in the early hours of the morning, when she felt a bit lonely, just for a chat with someone, and one of the order clerks who was very kind would talk to her for a while. Aunt Nan went deaf, too, and she had a very pretty tortoiseshell ear trumpet. Deafness runs in the Sowerby family. I now suffer from it, but technology has advanced so much since those days that it doesn't interfere with my life the way it did with the lives of poor Aunt Bella and Aunt Nan.

I don't ever remember the Levicks being asked to stay at Toddington Manor. They're not in any of the photographs I have of the big family gatherings there. I don't know whether they were left out because they were poor relations, or whether there was some embarrassment about Uncle George and Aunt Jeannie's adopted children Ruby and Gwen, whose birth certificates can't be traced. The Levicks were always in financial difficulties. We never used to visit them at their home but they often came to visit us. Gwen used to come with her man-friend to play bridge. Ruby's daughter Winifred used to come round, too, and my mother always seemed very sorry for Winifred. Sometimes Ma would ask me to look through my things to see if there were any clothes I could hand on to Winifred and I remember being quite cross about having to do that because I didn't want to give any of my stuff away.

I have a theory about who Ruby and Gwen were. Until we did the research for this book I didn't know they had no birth certificates in the names they were known by but, when I found that out, a lot of things made sense to me that hadn't made sense before. I think they were Ma's half-sisters and that she knew it, because she was always so kind to them and tried so hard to help them out with money and clothes. She was particularly fond of Gwen and, if Ma knew the truth about their birth, it might explain why she chose to include a sub-plot in her play *A Man and Some Women* about a child who's not being treated kindly by some of his relatives because of the irresponsible actions of his parents. I suppose it's possible Ruby and Gwen were the daughters of my mysterious Great-Uncle Charles who went to America (in which case they were Ma's cousins and not her half-sisters), but I think it's much more likely that my grandfather (Ma's father, John George Sowerby) had a relationship with someone when Granny Sowerby was taking a rest under doctor's orders between having children. It must have been very awkward for Ruby and Gwen without birth certificates they could produce in the names they were always known by. People often have to produce a birth certificate as a means of identification and they wouldn't have been able to do that.

In later life Ruby's daughter Winifred became really strange in her attitude to money. Whenever anyone died she would get in contact immediately to see if she had been left any money and then she'd get distraught if she was told she hadn't been left anything. She caused a great deal of annoyance and embarrassment to a lot of people doing that and I'm told she once made a scene in the big London branch of Coutts bank and accused them of withholding money that was rightfully hers. She got her man-friend to ring up my husband when Ma died and they as much as accused him of withholding money from her. Ian was always very easy-going but I've never seen him as angry as he was that day, and that phone call really made me resent the fact that my mother had promised that Winifred should have her diamond ring when she died. As it happened, it was a ring I would really have liked to have, but Ma had promised it to Winifred so of course despite Winifred's behaviour we honoured Ma's promise, even though the ring wasn't mentioned in Ma's will.

I didn't understand that attitude of Winifred's to money for a long time but I think I do now. After her mother Ruby died of tuberculosis in 1940, her father, architect Gervase Bailey, married again, and when he eventually died he left nothing to Winifred or her brother Christopher, saying they had had sufficient benefit from him during their lifetime. He made his second wife his main beneficiary and named his stepson as his executor. That must have been really hurtful for them and, if Winifred didn't actually see the will, she might well have gone to her grave thinking that her step-brother had cheated her out of a bequest from her father.

I only met my Aunt Helen, Ma's eldest sister, once, and I never met her husband, who the family called Uncle Lank despite his name being Reginald. Helen visited us just once after her husband died, and Ma and she went back together to Tyneside to visit the places they'd known when they were children. It was a bit of a disappointment for them because they found that the houses they knew in Gateshead had been demolished and the grounds had been built over. Helen seemed to me quite a fierce person and she wasn't nearly as attractive as Ma. It didn't help her appearance that she wore pince-nez either. It was surprising that Ma and Helen chose to visit the North East together because they'd never been close. Helen was always very jealous of Ma because Ma had been my grandfather's favourite and he'd made that quite obvious. Ma didn't like Helen either and in several of her children's stories there is a spiteful and badly behaved elder sister who eventually gets her comeuppance, but maybe that visit to the North East finally helped to heal the rift between Ma and Helen. After all, Ma hadn't wanted to be her father's favourite and the position my grandfather put her in landed her with all sort of financial burdens which Helen never had to deal with despite being the eldest daughter. Helen died not long after that visit to the North East with Ma.

Helen's son had died in tragic circumstances and her daughter, my cousin Dorothy, was a very strange woman. She had a fixed way of looking at people that was quite unnerving. She was close to my cousin Barbara Sawyer, Aunt Ruth's daughter, and Barbara ended up taking care of Dorothy in her old age. I think it was very sad that Dorothy's parents had refused to let her have medical treatment for her hormone deficiency. She might have had a very much more fulfilled life if they'd decided differently. And Uncle Lank's manipulation of the inquest process to cover up Hugh's suicide was a disgrace. Barbara told me about it, and Ma said that Hugh had committed suicide too. I'm glad I never met Uncle Lank. I'm sure I wouldn't have liked him.

I didn't like Barbara's mother, my Aunt Ruth, either. She did such harm to my cousin Barbara by having Barbara's headmistress tell her of her father's death, not visiting or writing to Barbara about it, and then never allowing her father to be spoken of again. Barbara adored her father who was very gentle and kind, and Aunt Ruth knew how much Barbara loved him. Barbara was a trained nurse with a good career but when Aunt Ruth got older she made Barbara give it all up and come home to look after her, and after her mother died Barbara went north to Grange-over-Sands and looked after our cousin Dorothy. Barbara spent her whole life taking care of people. She never had any freedom or fun at all and she never married. Her mother saw to that.

I was always in awe of Ma's mother, Granny Sowerby. Once when I'd gone to stay with her when I was about five she asked me what I wanted for tea and I said tomato sandwiches. I was a London child and I didn't know anything about fruit and vegetables. I'd had strawberries before and liked them so, when Nanny and I had walked past a greengrocer's shop, I thought tomatoes would taste like strawberries because they were a similar colour. Granny sent out especially for some tomatoes and I took one bite of one sandwich and started to cry. When I explained what was the matter Nanny was sent for and that was the end of my tea with Granny Sowerby. I've never liked tomatoes since. And I remember one day when we were discussing *Rutherford & Son* (and the character of Janet who has an affair with her father's foreman) I said to Granny that perhaps someone in the Sowerby family had had an affair. Granny was scandalised! But I've always thought that might be true.

Visiting Aunt Marjory was alright as I always went with Nanny so I had no problems with Uncle Frank and Aunt Marjory was nice. But Barbara told me that she sometimes felt very awkward when she visited Aunt Marjory because she had to go by herself. Apparently Uncle Frank could be a bit of a nuisance but I don't think he meant any harm, or Ma wouldn't have let me go there.

I saw a lot of Aunt Mill of course because she was always visiting us and she worked very closely with Ma over the children's books. No one in the family realised that Aunt Mill was as talented as she was or that her illustrations and paintings would one day become so highly prized. Everyone underestimated her. Aunt Mill was just regarded as a funny little spinster and in the family people rather laughed at her. Aunt Mill became ill once and came to stay with us at 18 Kensington Square till she got better, but she showed no signs of getting better because she wanted to stay. She stayed and stayed until Pa put his foot down and finally she went back to her home.

When Aunt Mill died, Ma cleared out Aunt Mill's little flat in Bina Gardens and Helen's daughter Dorothy, who had been close to Aunt Mill, had most of Aunt Mill's stuff. Unfortunately some time later Dorothy and my cousin Barbara gave away a lot of Aunt Mill's paintings and made a bonfire of her little drawings because they had no idea they were valuable. I was really angry when I found out, but it was too late. Barbara's response when I rang her up about it was, "Well, you can't keep everything."

Pa and Ma had a wonderful social life and I hope that having me didn't interfere with it as much as they thought it might. They had many friends from the literary and theatre world so we had lots of interesting visitors in addition to family visitors. Ma must have inherited all Pa's friends when they got married and Pa's friends from the Garrick Club and from *Punch* often came to dinner. EV Knox, the owner of *Punch,* visited us regularly and so did Kenneth Bird, who was the artist Fougasse, who did all the wonderful wartime posters for *Careless Talk Costs Lives.* He was a lovely man and gave me a couple of small pictures which I still have. Pa knew AA Milne, who wrote *Winnie the Pooh,* because they both wrote for *Punch,* and EH Shepard, who did the illustrations for *Winnie the Pooh* (and for Kenneth Grahame's *Wind in the Willows*) also knew Pa through working for *Punch* magazine. Other friends of my parents who came to dinner regularly were the writer Ian Hay, and the stage and film actors Allan Aynesworth, Leslie Banks and Godfrey Tearle, and Mrs Patrick Campbell was one of our neighbours in Kensington Square.

Pa was also a member of the Dramatists' Club, which started off as a kind of trade union for playwrights but ended up just as a lunch club. George Bernard Shaw was a member, too, and so was the actor and theatre manager Granville Barker. Ma had been very cross when Granville Barker turned down her play *A Man and Some Women* in 1914, but they stayed friends even after he left the theatre shortly after that. The comment in his letter to her at the time about men being drawn back to their homes is really ironic given that not long after writing it he left his first wife, the actress Lillah

McCarthy, for a wealthy twice-married American 12 years his senior called Helen Huntington. Granville Barker often came to dinner with us with Helen. Their coal black chow chow dog had an emerald green harness and lead, and he always had to be one of the guests too. He was a gorgeous dog.

Cyril Hogg, the owner of Samuel French & Co, was a close friend of my parents. He handled my mother's plays personally and they weren't promoted nearly so actively once Cyril Hogg had died. I think that's one of the reasons her plays faded from public memory for a time before being re-discovered in the 1980s. Cyril Hogg lived not far away in Holland Park and he often used to call at the house in his Rolls Royce. I remember Ma once patting the bonnet of his car and saying that some of her money went to buy him things like that. Cyril had a bit of a reputation with the ladies and it was said that you could always tell when he'd been a bit naughty because he would buy a nice present for his wife Cicely. Cyril used to pick me up at the local bus stop and give me a lift until my parents found out and put a stop to it. It was the usual thing from Ma – "You'll get a name." It was quite unnecessary because there was nothing in it. He was only being kind, and anyway I could take care of myself.

Because they were older parents, Ma and Pa's ideas about what I should and shouldn't be allowed to do were drawn from the previous century when they were growing up, and they just couldn't get their heads around the fact that life in the 1930s was different. It was always "You'll get a name." The mother of one of my friends once offered to take me on a holiday abroad with her and her daughter but Ma even said No to that. That time the reason was that "Something might happen." I can't imagine what.

Ma and Pa always listened to classical music in the house and I remember asking Pa why they never put on any dance music. I had a little turntable gramophone in my bedroom and Pa said it was bad enough hearing that noise coming from my bedroom without their playing dance music downstairs as well. Still, that's normal, I suppose. Most parents find their children's choice of music not to their taste.

If I was going out I would creep downstairs in the hope of getting out of the house without my parents hearing me but most of the time Pa would spot me and come to check my appearance before I left the house. He would always insist that I put on a hat and gloves, and took off my lipstick. So I did as I was asked and as soon as I got round the corner I took off the hat and gloves and put my lipstick back on again. I had a choice between deceiving my parents or looking ridiculous in front of my friends. I chose the former, but it made me feel very uncomfortable.

By the time I was 17 and plans were afoot for me to be a debutante Pa was 66 and Ma 59. The whole debutante thing bored Ma to tears but I had to be a debutante because all my friends were going to be presented and socially it would have been disastrous for me if I hadn't been, too. It was just an automatic thing that everybody did. During the previous year there were lunches and teas at which the mothers all consulted with one another about the dates when the dances, balls and other formal events would be held, and they all made lists of all the people who needed to be invited to all the events. But as Ma had never been presented as a girl she couldn't be there when I was actually presented in 1936 so Pa got his cousin Nick's wife Frances to see to that part of it. I don't think Ma minded not going to the garden party at the Palace – I think she was glad to be out of it. That kind of event really wasn't her scene at all, but she was keen for everything to be right for me socially.

All the dances were really good social training. When you arrived at the door your name was announced, and you had to make a proper entrance all on your own to a room full of grandly dressed people, most of whom you didn't know. When I was going to a dance my mother would see me into a taxi and then go home to bed. If the hostess wasn't arranging taxis to see us home at the end of the dance, Ma would get up again at 1am and come and fetch me. When I saw her standing in the doorway looking stern I would dive into the crowd and hide so she wouldn't see me straight away, but of course in the end I had to leave my friends and go home with her.

Ma had no idea what we used to get up to. If the dance wasn't particularly good we would all go to a great night club called the Florida. There was a revolving dance floor there and little tables with telephones on them, so you could telephone someone you saw who you liked the look of, and then dance with them. We all made sure we got back to the dance at about midnight so our parents never knew that we'd been at a night club for most of the evening instead of the dance where they thought we were. One night when we left a night club – this time it was the 400 Club – the girls including me were all wearing very full skirts so we danced the Can-Can in Leicester Square, and all the taxi drivers applauded. My mother would have been absolutely horrified if she'd known.

One evening a couple of years later when a boyfriend saw me home after a party I asked him in to the dining-room for a coffee at about 1am and suddenly Pa charged in through the door in his dressing-gown armed with a knuckle-duster. Then he saw it was me. "Oh, I'm sorry," he said, "I thought you were burglars." And he went back to bed. My boyfriend was astonished and said, "Does your father often do that?" Why on earth Pa should have kept knuckle-dusters in the house I've no idea.

And a year or so after that, just before the war, Ian saw me home and Ma called out of the window to me and asked if Ian was with me. I said, "Yes." It was about 2am. Ma said to Ian, "Well, you'd better phone your parents. They're waiting up for you." Apparently Ian's parents had phoned Ma and asked if she wasn't worried because I wasn't home. "No, should I be?" Ma responded. Ian came into the house and rang his parents and he was furious with them for doing that. It was ridiculous. He was 23 years old!

If it hadn't been for the Second World War I don't think Ian and I would have got married, as he was supposed to go out to India with his brother and start work there. He was actually born in India. However, because the war had started he couldn't go. Ma didn't want us to get married. She liked Ian but she didn't like his parents. Ma and Pa accepted our getting married in the end but the atmosphere was always pretty frosty between my parents and my in-laws, who in any case didn't like me and disapproved of my parents as theatre people.

Ian and I got married in November 1939 and within four years I'd had Michael and then Nigel, I know now that I was much too immature to be a parent and because I'd been brought up by a nanny I was totally unprepared for motherhood. I'd been spoilt, I suppose, and I hadn't ever had to take much responsibility until I had the boys. Apart from working for MI5 at the start of the war, once I'd been presented I'd just been allowed to have a good time and enjoy myself with an allowance from my parents, and I thought I still ought to be out enjoying myself. I absolutely hated being stuck at home with two small children and I couldn't wait for them to be old enough for us to send them off the boarding-school. They went there when they were eight years old and luckily they really enjoyed it.

Ma loved being a grandmother and Ma's cook Florence adored Michael and Nigel, too. Florence looked just like a cottage-loaf and the boys were always welcome in her kitchen, and Ma was excellent with children provided she had no parental responsibility for them so she was wonderful with Michael and Nigel. I was amazed when a friend of mine who used to live near us in Kensington Square told me her three children often used to go and knock at Ma's door and ask to go in to play in her house instead of playing in Kensington Square Gardens. Apparently they absolutely loved being with Ma. It's so ironic and so desperately sad that the only child she couldn't get close to was her own daughter.

In 1952 the BBC Home Service broadcast an edited version of *Rutherford & Son* and Ma went to see Sir Lewis Casson to discuss her ideas about how the play should be performed. They got on all right together but Ma didn't feel Sir Lewis had really taken to her ideas. He had his own views about *Rutherford & Son* and wasn't very receptive to the views of the playwright. Ma was very anxious for me to listen to the play on the radio because *Rutherford & Son* had been a success before I was born, but unfortunately I forgot it was on and I missed it. She was very disappointed, and I've often wondered whether that was the reason she thought I wasn't interested in her work. That wasn't true. I was. I would love to see a really good production of *Rutherford & Son*. I've never seen one yet that matched the way I think it ought to be performed. The best production I saw was the one directed by Wyn Jones at the New End Theatre in Hampstead in 1988. It's a tiny theatre and they had a properly cluttered Victorian set which gave the play just the right oppressive atmosphere. I didn't like the National Theatre production in 1994 – the Cottesloe stage looked bigger than it is because there wasn't much on it. And the set was all wrong. I kept getting phone calls from friends telling me how awful that production was. *Rutherford & Son* is a naturalistic play and it needs a naturalistic set.

When Pa was in his eighties he became seriously deaf and then he became very difficult to deal with. He'd always had a short fuse but his deafness infuriated him so much that he had no patience at all. And he was bored. He had nothing to do because *Punch* no longer wanted his poetry. Then he was killed at the railway crossing in Egham. Even more than 50 years later I find that difficult to talk about. I loved him so much.

I don't think Ma really changed particularly after Pa died, apart perhaps from becoming more peaceful. She remained very fit. Michael and Nigel kept in close contact with her, and I made sure she had someone resident to look after her. Miss Innes was a brick to put up with Ma, who showed no appreciation at all of anything she did, but when Miss Innes died it was really difficult. One night we had a telephone call from the police to say Miss Innes had dropped dead in the Gloucester Road when she was out shopping and Ma wouldn't open the door to the police so she still didn't know what had happened. We got dressed and after banging on her door for a long time Ma came and said quite crossly that she wasn't going to stay up till Miss Innes got home. I told her Miss Innes was ill and in hospital but in point of fact she was already dead. I slept that night on the couch.

I eventually found someone to live in and take care of Ma, but I didn't really trust the woman and after that I checked on things every single day. Ma stayed physically fit but she did get a bit forgetful and would think we hadn't been to see her for weeks when I'd had lunch with her the day before. I couldn't believe it when she told me she'd destroyed all her letters and photographs, because she'd previously asked me to promise to destroy her love letters after her death and I'd agreed. It made me feel that she didn't trust me not to read her private letters, and I would never have done such a thing.

And destroying the photographs was a terrible thing to do. All our history was gone. But Ma was convinced that no one was interested in her work and achievements any more, and especially me. I was very hurt.

Even though she was 93, it was still a shock when Ma died. She hadn't been ill and I just didn't expect it. I remember meeting her for lunch not long before she died. Everyone used to meet up in Harrods Bank. I was sitting there waiting for her as usual and I can still see her now, striding across the bank towards me.

I wish Ian, Michael and Nigel could have contributed their thoughts to this book, but Ian died in 1982, Michael in 1996 and Nigel in 2000. Ma now has four great-grandchildren and seven great-great-grandchildren but our branch of the Sowerbys has died out in this country and in Canada, because Lawrence's two sons died without having had any male children and no one else had sons to carry on the Sowerby name. But it's wonderful, now that we've found Lawrence's descendants, to have copies of all the old family photographs that had been lost to us for so long, and to know that our Canadian cousins really value their family history so much.

Ma would be astonished at the lives her descendants live today and she would probably be very shocked at how much freedom children have compared with when she was young. But she would be very pleased that her plays are still remembered and valued because she died believing that no one was interested in her work and achievements.

I wish I could have got close to Ma in the way my boys were able to do. If only Ma could have hugged me even once, or just relaxed her guard long enough to look at me without judging what she saw, then perhaps I could have got past that wall that Ma spent her whole life hiding behind. But she never did. She couldn't even tell me that she'd realised she'd been too old-fashioned in the way she brought me up. She wrote a play about it instead. And I believe that Ma was writing to herself when she wrote her poem, *To A Woman I Know*:

What will you dream of when your life
Is gay with light and laughter
When joy is yours to take or leave
With gold to follow after
When all your little world is bright
With stars and candles gleaming –
What will you dream of when the night
Has left you time for dreaming?

What will you dream of last of all
When you are done with living,
And all the smiles you gave the world
Seem scarcely worth the giving?
The little more you never gave
Lest pain should come too near you –
The foolish thing you never said
Lest love should overhear you.[65]

"The little more you never gave lest pain should come too near you." That was my mother. I loved Ma but I don't think she ever really believed that. And I never felt that her love of me was unconditional.

I'm going to have Ma's poem *To A Woman I Know*[66] read at my funeral.

Joan Smith
London, 2009

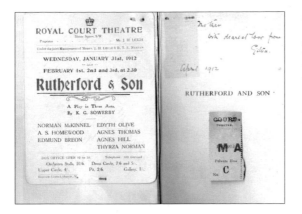

'By KG Sowerby': the producers still suggesting male authorship, even after Githa's true identity was known. Programme and ticket for performance of *Rutherford & Son* at the Royal Court Theatre on 1 February 1912, found pinned into a first edition of *Rutherford & Son* dedicated by Githa to her mother.

John Sowerby (1808 1879)

The farmhouse at Netherton, Cumbria, 2008 (photo: Tom Cruikshanks)

Shipcote Farm, Gateshead, c1939 (photo: Gateshead Central Library)

Katherine Githa Sowerby, c1900

Shipcote House, c1880 (photo: Gateshead Central Library)

Benwell Towers, Newcastle-upon-Tyne

Servants at Ravenshill

John George Sowerby's studio

Newspaper ad for Sowerby's Ellison Glass Works

Whitehill Cottage in Chester-le-Street
(photo: Chester-le-Street Heritage Group)

High Level Bridge and New Stourbridge Glass Works
(see detail, left), c1840

Anne Robson Sowerby, c1860

Isabella Sowerby, 1863

Martha Sowerby, 1869

John George Sowerby, c1870

Annie Elizabeth Sowerby, 1875

Charles Robson Sowerby, c1877

The Geography Lesson: illustration from *Young Maids and Old China*

The Attempt: illustration from *Come With Me*

Githa and Lawrence through their father's eyes. Frontispiece illustration for *At Home Again*

The Maidens and the Angler: illustration from *Come With Me*

Illustration from *At Home*

Play-Time: illustration from *Afternoon Tea*

The Spinet: illustration from *Young Maids and Old China*

The Bird-Catcher: illustration from *Afternoon Tea*

The Old Clock: illustration from *At Home Again*

Before Breakfast: illustration from *At Home Again*

Katherine Githa Sowerby

Githa's mother, Amy Margaret Sowerby, c1880

Marjory Gladys Sowerby

John Lawrence Sowerby

Rachel Ruth Sowerby

Amy Millicent Sowerby

Margaret Helen Sowerby

Hall Garth interior with James Guthrie portraits. The portrait of Margaret Helen Sowerby aged seven is on show at the National Gallery of Scotland but until this photograph was unearthed, the fact that James Guthrie had also been commissioned to paint John Lawrence Sowerby aged nine was not known. The present whereabouts of this portrait of Lawrence Sowerby is also not known

Hall Garth, Coatham Mundeville

The entrance to Hall Garth

Hall Garth interior

Field House, High Teams, Gateshead: c1890

Hall Garth interior

Margaret Helen Sowerby, c1900

Githa's brother, John Lawrence Sowerby, 1900

Lawrence's original cabin, 1913

Marjory Gladys Sowerby

Lawrence and Lucy
Sowerby, c1960

The house Lawrence
built for his family

Cover of *The Wise
Book*, Githa and
Millicent's first
children's book,
published in 1906
by JM Dent

Amy Millicent
Sowerby, c1920

Newspaper cutting: Captain John and Mrs Githa Kendall,
8 July 1912, snapped by a reporter as they leave their wedding

Newspaper cutting: John Kaye
Kendall: April 1912

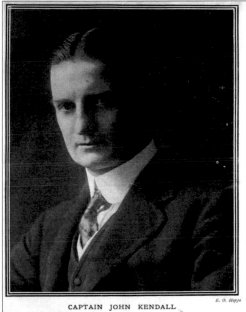

CAPTAIN JOHN KENDALL

Whose delightful new book, "Odd Numbers," is proving a tremendous
success. Captain Kendall was formerly in the Royal Artillery, and his
first literary work appeared in "The Times of India" thirteen years ago
over the pseudonym of "Dum-Dum," now a familiar landmark in the
pages of "Punch," to which he has contributed since 1902. On being
invalided home he found time for many humorous poems so well known
to "Punch" readers, and has also written three plays, "Mrs. Bill," a
three-act comedy, "Laughter in Court," and "Dad." His new book will
add greatly to his reputation as a writer of humorous verse

Newspaper cutting: John Kaye Kendall

Newspaper cutting: Githa
Sowerby: April 1912

The Dutch *Rutherford & Son* programme

Photograph of Githa's father John George Sowerby, c1910

Leaflet publicising the work of the War Supplies Depot, Kensington

Joan Kendall: c1928

Newspaper article on the production of *Sheila*

Githa and her daughter Joan, autumn 1918, at Little Chewton

Orde House, Whitchurch, Herefordshire, 2008 (photo: Mrs Barroll-Brown)

Toddington Manor, Winchcombe, Gloucestershire (photo: Adam Stanford/www.aerial-cam.co.uk)

Isabel May Buzzard

Isabella Andrews with some of the pugs: c1928

Studio portrait of Githa

Plaque at St Brevita Church, Lanlivery, Cornwall

The Heaven and Hell window, Toddington Manor

Toddington Manor interior photos
by kind permission of Damien Hirst

Main staircase,
Toddington Manor,
Winchcombe, Gloucestershire

CHAPTER EIGHT

Finding Githa through her plays

A personal view

The British theatre may have re-discovered *Rutherford & Son* and even hailed it as a classic, but Githa Sowerby's other plays are steadfastly ignored, largely because they are not published. Few people have ever heard of their titles – and, even if they have, not many people know where to obtain copies of the scripts or who administers the literary estate for Githa's plays.[67] In view of this fact, it seems appropriate to include here a more detailed overview of each of her plays.

In 1821 a glass curtain was constructed at the Coburg Theatre.[i] Made up of 63 pieces of looking-glass fitted together within a gilt frame, it was considered a marvel. When it reflected the front of the house, producing the illusion of a vast circle, the audience could look at themselves. When it was brought into use on the stage, it created a continuous space, making the members of the audience a part of the action.[68] Like that glass curtain, Githa's plays both reflected herself and, in her day, challenged her audiences in their view of themselves and their world.

Githa's plays are almost entirely set in the home (*The Stepmother* has one scene that takes place at Lois's place of work). Without exception, the male theatre critics of her day categorised her plays as family dramas, failing to recognise the political content at their heart. Ibsen's *A Doll's House* and *Hedda Gabler* had both been produced in London before Githa moved south, so it is not known whether she saw those plays before she wrote *Rutherford & Son*. However, she knew George Bernard Shaw and as a fellow Fabian she is likely to have been familiar with his book *The Quintessence of Ibsenism*[69]. Ibsen believed that social change should begin with individuals because power structures within the bourgeois family reflected the power structures within the wider society.[70]

"You've been here nigh on three months," Janet Rutherford tells her sister-in-law in *Rutherford & Son*. "If you think you're going to change this house with your soft ways, you're mistaken. Nothing'll change us now – nothing. We're made that way – set – and we've got to live that way."

---

i The Coburg became the Royal Victoria Hall, now known as the Old Vic.

Mary Rutherford – with the part she plays in the changes that begin to occur in the Rutherford household after her arrival – mirrors the role that Githa tried to fill as a dramatist in getting people to question the way society functioned. Like Ibsen, Githa believed that the power structures within the domestic setting reflected the hierarchical structures in the host society, and she considered that individuals, families and society all needed to change.

An analysis of the issues emerging from her plays point to the aspects of the society around her that Githa felt most strongly about. Five issues predominate – marriage, motherhood, class, sexual relationships, and propriety – closely followed by the need for women to achieve economic independence from men, the role of women in society, and fatherhood. (The inclusion of the theme of fatherhood, prompted no doubt by her personal experience with her own father, sets Githa apart from other feminist writers of her generation in her conviction that what we now call gender stereotyping was damaging to men as well as to women.)

It is interesting to note the issues that are *not* mentioned. Githa's plays do not deal with votes for women, party politics or war. Given that during her early career she was writing at the height of suffragette activity, the omission of the debate over votes for women is particularly significant. It suggests that Githa's analysis was broader than the campaign to secure women equal voting rights with men. Like fellow playwright and feminist author, Cicely Hamilton, she was much more interested in smashing the accepted stereotype of the 'womanly woman' than in the narrower cause of Votes for Women.

Githa's first attempts at play-writing appeared in print in 1910 when Hodder & Stoughton published her book *Little Plays for Little People* in Britain and America The book was one of a trio published that year, the other two being *Little Songs for Little People* and *Little Stories for Little People*.

Little Plays for Little People contains six short plays – *The Magic Word or Civility Costs Nothing, The Rose and the Ring, King Cophetua and the Beggar Maid, Fortunata and Cassandra, Bearskin,* and *Princess Tenderheart.* Like her father's children's books published 30 years earlier, these were commercial productions, fitted to the taste of the parents of the day: simple tales of magic in which, after trials and tribulations along the way, Good triumphs over Evil. Each play has between four and eight main characters supported by ladies in waiting, courtiers, customers in a market, etc, and have running times of between ten and 15 minutes. With their clear structures and simple dialogue, these little plays can easily be staged with the basic costumes and props available in schools, and no doubt were often used for that purpose both in England and America.[i]

Githa's children's books and her first plays were broadly conventional, lightened by a touch of her personal wit. Take a passage from her *King Cophetua and the Beggar Maid,* published in that first collection.

FIRST PAGE	The Princess is much too vain and proud to fall in love with anyone but herself. Besides, she doesn't know that Cophetua is a great king and the richest person in the world. The joke of it all is that she didn't know that the rose he sent her was a magic rose and simply thought that he was too poor to give her anything better.
SECOND PAGE	The King wants to be loved for himself alone, I suppose.

King Cophetua and the Beggar Maid, Act One[71]

Within a year, while floating in a punt on the sunny river Thames, the author of *King Cophetua* would be writing *Rutherford & Son* – that passionate denunciation of domestic tyranny and the destructive power of the worship of advancement and family name.

RUTHERFORD	What more did you want in God's name?
JANET	Oh, what more! The women down there know what I wanted, with their bairns wrapped in their shawls and their men to come home at night time. I've envied them – envied them their pain, their poorness – the very times they hadn't bread. Theirs isn't the dead empty house, the black o' the moors; they got something to fight, something to be feared of. They got life, those women we send cans o' soup to out o' pity when their bairns are born. Me, a lady! With work for a man in my hands, passion for a man in my heart. I'm common, common!
RUTHERFORD	It's a lie! I've risen up. You can't go back on it – my children can't go back.

Rutherford & Son, Act Two[72]

---

i *Little Plays for Little People* was sufficiently successful for Hodder & Stoughton to re-issue it in 1912 under the title *Little Plays for School and Home*, to capitalise on Githa's fame as the author of *Rutherford & Son.*

Rutherford & Son
First performed at the Royal Court Theatre, London, 31 January 1912

Throughout *Rutherford & Son* burns the issue of human sacrifice to the god of capitalism – as Janet puts it in her furious condemnation of her father: "You've ruined my life, you with your getting on…"

The influence of Ibsen in *Rutherford & Son* seems clear. For example, the positioning of the portrait of her father that dominates the stage in *Hedda Gabler* probably inspired the positioning of the portrait of the glassworks founder in *Rutherford & Son*, and the slamming of the outer door when Nora leaves her husband and children at the end of *A Doll's House* is echoed by the slamming offstage of the outer door when Janet leaves her home in *Rutherford & Son*.

The story is of a family imploding under the demands of the ambition of the capitalist tyrant and pater familias, John Rutherford. The younger members of the family resent being in thrall to the glassworks but Rutherford's children, John, Richard and Janet, still think nothing can change – every initiative is crushed by the ruthless head of the house. "No one ever stands out against father for long, you know that – or else they get so knocked about they don't matter any more." (Janet, Act One, *Rutherford & Son*)

In her 1909 book, *Marriage as a Trade,* Cicely Hamilton explored how economic and social forces had combined for generations to train women to fulfil one role only in society, that of wife and mother, in exchange for their board and keep, while at the same time ensuring that all other means of maintaining life were barred from them. (Githa may well have known actress, playwright, journalist and travel writer Cicely Hamilton, as they moved in similar social circles.) Like Hamilton, Githa Sowerby believed that the route to equality for women lay through the achievement of economic independence from men. But she was particularly conscious of the women who had little choice but to be dependent on men's money. In *Rutherford & Son*, the unmarried daughter Janet has been trapped like this for years as an unpaid and unappreciated housekeeper in her father's household. She achieves independence only when her father orders her out of the house because of her sexual relationship with Martin, the foreman of his glassworks. But, unlike her weakling brothers Richard and John, Janet does not leave defeated by domestic tyranny.

JANET　… You think you've done for me when you use shameful words on me and turn me out o' your house. You've let me out of gaol! Whatever happens to me now, I shan't go on living as I lived here.

Whatever Martin's done, he's taken me from you. You've ruined my life, you with your getting on. I've loved in wretchedness, all the joy I ever had made wicked by the fear o'you... Who are you? A man – a man that's taken power to himself, power to gather people to him and use them as he wills – a man that'd take the blood of life itself and put it into the Works – into Rutherford's. And what ha' you got by it – what? You've got Dick, that you've bullied till he's a fool – John, that's waiting for the time when he can sell what you've done – and you got me – me to take your boots off at night – to well nigh wish you dead when I had to touch you. Now! Now, you know!

Rutherford & Son, Act Two[73]

When journalist Keble Howard asked Githa about the characters of *Rutherford & Son* in his February 1912 interview, she turned aside his curiosity, asking why he should expect her to know any more about them than anyone else. It was natural that she should wish to protect the privacy of her family and she did so successfully, but the personal price paid for business success by members of the Sowerby family was real enough. Several of the characters in *Rutherford & Son* are drawn from Githa's family history. The domestic tyrant John Rutherford is based on Githa's grandfather, John Sowerby, who transformed the small struggling New Stourbridge Glass Works into the huge, market-leading Sowerby's Ellison Glass Works. But the economic situation confronting John Rutherford in the play is not that faced by Githa's grandfather, who was very successful and made huge profits. John Rutherford's problems are more akin to those faced in the next generation by Githa's father, John George Sowerby, who managed the glassworks when it had become a limited liability company and when it was trading under much more difficult market conditions than Githa's grandfather experienced. The opening set description of the play states, "From above the heavy polished sideboard the late John Rutherford looks down from his frame..." John Rutherford, the domestic tyrant of the play, is the *Son* of the play's title and not the *Rutherford*, which suggests that he has become what he is through the tyranny of an earlier generation. The portrait Githa was describing could have been a picture of her great-grandfather, George Sowerby – perhaps a portrait commemorating his year as Mayor of Gateshead from 1841-1842. Gateshead Council must at some time have possessed such a picture but it is not known what happened to it, and if the family had a portrait of Githa's great-grandfather it has since been lost.

The character of the old-fashioned and nagging Aunt Ann is probably based on Githa's grandmother Anne Robson Sowerby, who returned from living in London to die at Chollerton in 1896: she is the only elderly relative known to have been resident in a house in which Githa was also living. And the character of young John Rutherford seems to be based partly on Githa's brother Lawrence who, after planning to leave for some years, emigrated to Canada in 1912; and partly on her great-uncle Charles, who disappeared abroad to become a gold prospector some time between 1871 and 1890 and died in America. The reference in the play to young John attending Harrow for one year might be a reference to Lawrence's education at Winchester College but it seems more likely that Githa was thinking of her uncle Charles' attendance at Prestonville school in Hove, given old John Rutherford's comment in the play that young John was sent to Harrow for a year because he thought this would be better than the grammar school, but that he had been wrong.

According to her daughter, Githa herself did not have a Tyneside accent, but *Rutherford & Son* is written in Geordie dialect, some of it very broad indeed. A production of *Rutherford & Son* that remains true to the play's Tyneside roots requires all the characters except Mary to speak with Tyneside accents, while Mary speaks with a working-class London accent. If a production is to be historically correct, the play should be set after 1875 because of contemporary developments in company law. Limited liability companies did not come into existence until 1875. This was the law under which John Rutherford, like Githa's father, is forced to deal with a board of directors instead of pleasing himself about how the company is to be run. And the registration of patents about which John Rutherford speaks was not possible before 1870. Other details, too, fit with 1875 as the approximate date when the action of the play takes place. The references to the local interest in competitive running could well be Githa's way of disguising references to her father's involvement in competitive rowing in the 1870s, a high point of enthusiasm for this sport on Tyneside. There's a reference to one of the competitors being overtrained for a race, which echoes a problem that occurred when one of Tyneside's most famous oarsmen overtrained his son.

In the stage directions at the start of Act One, Githa explains that the family speaks of John Rutherford "going across" to the glassworks from his home[74] This could either refer to her father John George Sowerby "going across" the footbridge from Ravenshill on Low Fell to Sowerby's Ellison Glass Works in Gateshead, or to his father John Sowerby "going across" the Tyne to the glassworks from his home at Benwell Towers in the village of Benwell, Newcastle. However, as Githa makes it clear that the house in the play is very uncomfortable; this is more likely to be inspired by her grandfather's home at Benwell Towers rather than the luxurious Ravenshill. The place name Grantley is probably a pseudonym for Gateshead, where both the New Stourbridge Glass Works and later Sowerby's Ellison Glass Works stood.

In the play, once change begins it cannot be stopped. Class distinction destroys a relationship that could have brought happiness to Martin and Janet. The Rutherford household has no choice but to adapt, as one by one John Rutherford's children leave the house. In different ways they are all wounded, but they escape their ultimate fate of death under the wheels of Moloch[i]. Janet will live and work in a district where she is not known so that the scandal of her sexual relationship with a working man will not follow her. Richard, a clergyman, will accept the post of curate in a distant parish away from his father's undermining of his ministry. Feckless young John Rutherford, having failed to sell his father his invention of a new formula for producing white metal[ii] more cheaply, steals money from his father's desk. When he refuses to replace the money, his wife Mary realises that she is better off without him, and he accepts with alacrity her suggestion that he leave to seek his fortune in Canada without her and the baby.

With Janet's words of hate and scorn still ringing in his ears, old John Rutherford sits alone but for his despised working-class daughter-in-law. But, for the first time in his life, the tyrant has met his match. His gentle daughter-in-law Mary gains his grudging respect as she proves that a woman can be quite as ruthless as a man when fighting for the future of her baby. Mary, gambling that her father-in-law will be too old in ten years' time to cause his grandson any harm, takes control of her future by offering him her baby son Tony to train up to run the glassworks, in return for their keep, on condition that John Rutherford leaves in her sole control of her son's upbringing until then. She takes little joy in the prospect of the barren life she faces but she reasons that it will give her baby a better chance than anything she could offer him independently. Forced in spite of himself to respect Mary's courage and strength, John Rutherford accepts her terms. The play ends with the cry of the waking baby.

In *Rutherford & Son*, Githa set a pattern she was to follow in all but one of her adult plays (the exception being *Direct Action*). In contrast to the neat 'happy ending' conventions of her day, she leaves the audience with questions. Was Mary right effectively to 'sell' her baby to her father-in-law? Will Moloch grind a new generation beneath its wheels or will Mary teach her father-in-law new ways in time to save her son from the fire god of the Canaanites? And the question that drives the whole play – is the price of capitalism too high?

---

i Moloch: a pagan god or demon that demanded human sacrifices. See Preface.

ii The word 'metal' is used in the industry to refer to glass, so the new formula for "white metal" devised by young John Rutherford refers to a new formula for the production of clear glass.

Before Breakfast
First performed at the Playhouse Theatre, London, 2 May 1912

Before Breakfast is a one-act comedy, a curtain-raiser, written largely in
Cockney dialect. It invites the audience to have a laugh at the expense of
armchair socialists. While demonstrating Githa's sense of humour and her
deft touch in writing in a dialect quite different from that of her native
Tyneside, the piece presents a comical picture of the 'idle classes' that no
doubt amused her Fabian friends. It was produced in London in 1912 at the
same time as the dark and brooding *Rutherford & Son*, and provides a striking
contrast in tone.

The play is set in the Linton family's fashionable home in Belgrave Square.
There are four characters – a housekeeper (Mrs Gray), a butler (Snee), a
housemaid (Jinny), and George Linton, the rich young son of the house who,
much to his family's dismay, wishes to marry a music hall actress.

SNEE   … It's my opinion Mr George's no more in love than I am.
            But there's the master a-standing on the 'earthrug a-telling
            him about the family honour, and 'er ladyship a-talking fit to
            weary a saint – it's only a-drivin' 'im to marry 'er.
MRS GRAY   It all comes of young gentlemen taking up with these new-
            fangled ideas – Socialism or whatever they call it.
SNEE   No, Mrs Gray, that's where you're wrong. They gets sweet on
            the young woman first – afterwards the Socialism takes 'em.

            Before Breakfast[75]

The actress has wooed George under a false name and told him a hard
luck story; they are to be married secretly later that week. From George's
description of his girl's role when the actress played the Carrot in a musical
hall vegetable act, Jinny the housemaid realises that he is talking about
her sister Cissy. She tells George the truth. Appalled, George gets Jinny to
answer when his fiancée telephones.

JINNY   Mr George Linton says e's gone out – what? Yes, it's me
            and no error…Jinny, Jinny, swallow and get it over! I'm in
            a place 'ere. It's no use arguin' about it – it'll only spoil the
            telephone…Your language is disgustin'… I tell you 'e's out
            – I tell you – what? Liar yourself. Who borrowed money off
            mother and never paid 'er back? Who walked out with the
            sweep? What? Boil your own 'ead and boil it 'ard!

            Before Breakfast[76]

By the end of this speech, George is a socialist no more. He tips Jinny a sovereign to commemorate "the day when we both forgot our place" and flees the house for an undisclosed destination in the African jungle.

A Man and Some Women
First performed at the Gaiety Theatre, Manchester, October 1914

Impressed by the talent for comedy Githa displayed in *Before Breakfast*, her agents at Curtis Brown urged her to write a full-length comedy – a desirable commodity in the 1913 theatre marketplace. Githa did not follow their advice. Following on from *Rutherford & Son* she wished to pursue the theme of domestic tyranny and the effects of female economic dependence from a different angle. The result was *A Man and Some Women*, an unjustly neglected play that is the soul-mate to *Rutherford & Son*.

In a twist to Githa's first subject, in *A Man and Some Women* the victim of domestic tyranny is a man whose persecutors are dependent females. The play is set in London. Richard Shannon longs to leave his partnership in a business in which he has no interest so he can take up a post as scientific adviser to a research project in Brazil. But he feels himself duty-bound to remain to support his wife and two unmarried sisters. In this there are echoes of Elizabeth Baker's 1907 play *Chains*, in which Charley Wilson also feels himself unable to seek his fortune in Canada because he is married and his wife is expecting a child. However, in Baker's play the marriage is a loving one. In *A Man and Some Women* there is no love between Richard and his wife. Hilda sees her husband solely as a provider of money and she has long ago ceased to pretend otherwise. There are elements of Githa's mother, the "icily regular, splendidly null" Amy Margaret Sowerby, in the character of Hilda – the mother with little interest in children and who is more concerned with social status and a privileged lifestyle than her husband's happiness or fulfilment.

Richard has two sisters – one, Elizabeth, intelligent but lazy, and the other sister, Rose, prim, stupid and spiteful. His sisters and wife are contrasted with a New Woman, his cousin Jessica Hildred, who earns her own living and relates to Richard as an equal. Richard's patience finally snaps when Rose accuses him of having an affair with Jessica and giving her money that was rightfully theirs. He tells the three female parasites that there is no money, that they have been living for the last ten years on his charity. At the same time he reveals that he has been supporting their recently deceased mother ever since she lost her money through an unwise investment. So instead of the bequest his sisters have been expecting, they will receive nothing, for their mother had nothing to leave.

ROSE	You ought to be ashamed of yourself. You're simply bullying.
RICHARD	For once in your life you've had the truth.
ROSE	You've insulted us all. We're women, your wife and sisters, and you've spoken to us as if we were men.
RICHARD	Oh, you're women – that's your defence. I've kept you because you're women – I've held my tongue because you're women. I bully you! You're the bullies, with your infernal nagging. I've stood it for ten years and I'll stand it no longer.
HILDA	Where are you going?
RICHARD	Out of it! Out of it!
ELIZABETH	Now you've done it!

A Man and Some Women, Act Two [77]

Facing reality for the first time, Elizabeth recounts to Jessica her experience of attending the Women's Work Bureau in search of a job.

JESSICA	You're going to work?
ELIZABETH	If anyone's fool enough to take me on. A nice time I had of it. I was given a paper, a form, which I was expected to fill out. What sort of post I wanted – I didn't know. What wages – I didn't know. My capabilities – I haven't any. I never felt such a fool in my life. There was a woman at the desk, quite a pleasant woman, and I loathed her so I could have hit her. I told her the best thing I could do was to apply to a Servants' Registry. At least I'm sober and honest.
JESSICA	Yes.
ELIZABETH	It's all very well for women who have been trained – but what good am I? I haven't been out of bed before ten for years.

A Man and Some Women, Act Three [78]

Githa's point was to highlight what it really meant to keep women at home in a state of idleness. Instead of being self-sacrificing, spiritual and pure the "some women" in *A Man and Some Women* are shown to be idle, grasping, selfish and ignorant – unsurprisingly, for they are no better than spoilt children. This cause and effect had first been exposed as early as 1792 in Mary Wollstonecraft's *Vindication of the Rights of Women*, and discussed again in works such as John Stuart Mill's 1869 essay *The Subjection of Women*. However, the consequences of keeping women in a state of "perpetual childhood" to preserve the illusion of male superiority was a novel theatrical subject in 1914. Audiences watching *A Man and Some Women* were challenged with the idea that Hilda, Rose and Elizabeth had become the malevolent creatures that they were because they had never in their lives had to take an ounce of responsibility for their own actions or been treated as being capable of doing so. Like Ibsen's Nora (though totally unlike her in personality), these three women are dolls in a doll's house.[79] And Richard Shannon is as trapped as Janet in *Rutherford & Son* – he too is a prisoner in the doll's house and needs to escape to find himself.

It is apparent from the detailed stage directions that Githa had a very clear picture in her mind of the characters she was portraying in *A Man and Some Women*. For example, she describes Rose as having:

> "… a face that is alternately watchful and foolish. She is constantly finding herself out of her depth and her efforts to keep herself afloat in general conversation have given her an air of petulance. As far as her appearance goes, she has evidently given herself up as a matter of conscience years ago, and her black dress is neither pretty nor ugly, but probably what some moderately inexpensive dressmaker thought suitable."

This description of Rose is reminiscent of Githa's youngest sister Ruth, who was selfish, demanding and not particularly bright. The character of Elizabeth is brighter and a much nicer person than her sister Rose, but she is lazy. Elizabeth may have been based on Githa's cousin Violet MacLean, daughter of Githa's uncle and aunt Sir Francis and Lady MacLean, who was pleasant and well liked but never needed to work because of the wealth and social position of her parents.

Githa adds a sub-plot involving nine-year-old Jack, Jessica's nephew, in which she touches on the injustice of blaming children for their parents' infringement of society's moral codes. Jack's mother has left her irresponsible husband and run off to Italy with another man. Richard wants to adopt Jack but Hilda and his sisters are against it, suggesting the boy is morally tainted by his mother's misdeeds. Not surprisingly once Richard has left his wife and sisters, Jack runs away to Jessica. By the end of the play Richard and Jessica have admitted that they love each other but Jessica refuses to become yet another in the long line of demanding women (starting with his mother, going on to a mistress and ending with his wife and two unmarried sisters) who have trapped and victimised Richard throughout his life. Jessica takes on the care of Jack herself leaving Richard free to accept the Brazil post. Like Nora in *A Doll's House*, Richard can now find out who he really is and what he truly wants in life, away from the domination of women.

As before, Githa leaves the audience with questions. Will Richard ever return from Brazil? If he does return to England, will he have matured to the point where he and Jessica could be happy together in a relationship of equals? And, given that Hilda is unlikely to divorce him, what kind of a life could Richard and Jessica build for themselves and Jack if they are not free to marry? But of vastly greater importance is the question that lies behind the whole play – for how much longer will society continue to assign child status to adult women and pay the heavy price for it?

The reversal of roles in a plot about domestic tyranny and what economic dependence can lead to was a bold idea. It must have taken audiences by surprise during its brief run at the Gaiety Theatre in Manchester in October 1914, but sadly no reviews have survived. The newspapers were too preoccupied with the war. And *A Man and Some Women* has been ignored since, apart from one revival in Bristol in 1996.

Sheila
First performed at St James's Theatre, London, 7 June, 1917

"One wonders what sort of generation of women that would be which grew from childhood to maturity unhampered and unhindered by the tradition of its own essential inferiority to the male half of humanity," wrote Cicely Hamilton in *Marriage as a Trade*.[80] By the time Githa Sowerby was writing *Sheila* in 1917, members of the women's movement were full of hope. Considerable advances had been made in the sphere of women's employment but class distinction was a more stubborn proposition to defeat. Equality in marital relationships was always going to require adjustments in the sensitive area of husbands' and wives' differing expectations of marriage. In *Sheila*, Githa Sowerby turned her attention to the added complication of class distinctions.

Once again, Githa drew on the experiences of people around her. As she could not type, Githa would take her handwritten scripts to shorthand and typewriting agencies such as Ethel Christian's in the Strand. In her regular visits she got to know the office staff who did her work. *Sheila* revolves around the story of two such working women. Githa describes the first secretary, Miss Bradley:

> "She is typing rapidly and monotonously from a reporter's shorthand-book propped open beside her. She is a sharp-tongued, business-like, kind-hearted little woman with a mouth that has grown thin through a long habit of concentration, and that rather pathetic air of undevelopment – a sort of arresting girlishness – which sometimes hangs about the unmarried woman of 40. She has pretty hair. Her dress is of grey alpaca, with a narrow white collar and a shiny black leather belt; she has a fountain pen pinned to her blouse and she wears a pair of Holland sleeves up to the elbows to keep her cuffs clean."[81]

The second secretary is the 'Sheila' of the play's title.

> "A pretty girl who will be a beautiful woman. Your first thought of her is to wonder how on earth she is a typist at twenty-five shillings a week – she is so obviously unbusiness-like. She is dressed in a navy blue cotton frock, which she has tried to make pretty with a cheap lacy collar and a bow at the throat. She too wears Holland sleeves."

Miss Bradley and Sheila have achieved economic independence but they are certainly not yet "unhampered and unhindered by the tradition of [their] own essential inferiority to the male half of humanity"[82]. Miss Bradley, the successful secretary of a publisher, explains to Sheila that she broke off her engagement years before because she could not respect a man who did not earn more than she did. And Sheila, her assistant, doesn't want to be economically independent; she aspires to the life of a wife with a husband who loves and takes care of her. She bursts into tears when the requirement to do some overtime prevents her going to the picture palace to see *Romeo and Juliet*.

Their employer, Mark Holdsworth, wants a son. He decides he is sufficiently in love with pretty Sheila to ignore her working-class origins and he asks her to marry him. Sheila decides she is in love with Mark and accepts. However, Sheila finds the reality of coping with her new husband's aristocratic relatives Lord and Lady Carden and their daughter Sybil, along with his other upper class friends, means that marriage to Mark is not the blissful dream she imagined. She is made to feel out place and a fool and she doesn't know "how to behave" in her new environment.

SHEILA   ... I was expected to make friends, I suppose. I didn't. I was too frightened to begin with, and I made a stupid sort of blunder – you'll laugh – I don't understand about titles and I thought it was correct to call her Lady James. Then there were several men there and I – – – I shook hands with them all round when they were introduced. The other women bowed. Then everything went wrong. I suppose I talked too much at dinner, anyway towards the end I found half the table listening to me and looking amused – – – and Mark was laughing – – – That finished me – – – I talked and talked, I simply had to – – – and by the time we got into the drawing-room I didn't care what happened.

Sheila, Act Two[83]

Then Sheila learns that, before he proposed, Mark told his cousin Sybil that he had decided to marry because he wanted a son. Feeling degraded and used,

Sheila leaves the house and goes abroad without telling him she is pregnant. When she eventually returns many months later, Mark and Sheila realise that they do genuinely love one another, but what would otherwise be a joyful reunion is tempered by suffering, as their baby son has died at birth.

Githa provides deft comic touches to highlight the darker passages of the play. Her description of the grumpy Sir James and Lady Carden suggests they were modelled on Githa's dog-breeding aunt and industrialist uncle, Isabella and Hugh Andrews. By the time *Sheila* was produced at St James's Theatre in 1917, Hugh Andrews was 85, so there was little danger of Githa's Aunt Bella and her Uncle Hugh coming all the way to London from Gloucestershire to witness themselves impersonated on stage. In her stage directions, Githa describes her characters:

> "Sir James... is a distinguished-looking unreasonable old man with a short abrupt manner which becomes hectoring on the smallest provocation. His wife is a gentle, old-fashioned, perfectly tactless woman... [whose] energies have all been absorbed in the effort to keep her husband in good humour."

When the pair first enter, Mark Holdsworth greets Lady Mary with, "How are the pugs?" Sir James is depicted as quarrelsome, unreasonable and money-mad. Lady Mary complains to her husband that she can't understand why he's so keen to make more money when they already have more than they know how to spend. "I'm sure if it weren't for the pugs and the Vicar's Easter offering I don't know how I should get through my allowance."

The male critics did not understand *Sheila*. One probably spoke for them all when he sneered: "The motive for the misunderstanding is too slender and too far-fetched for a mere man."[84] Reviewers complained about the death of Mark and Sheila's baby as if it was bad taste in a love story – yet the death is essential to Githa's proposition that for a man to choose a wife as one would a breeding animal and for a woman to choose a husband purely as a meal ticket is toxic for both sides and incompatible with equality in marital relationships. It does not seem too much of a stretch to perceive echoes of Ibsen again in this ending. At the end of A *Doll's House*, Nora leaves her husband and children, having said that she and Torvald Helmer would both have to change fundamentally for their husband and wife relationship ever to work. In *Sheila*, husband and wife come back together having accomplished those changes, but the baby born of their unequal relationship has died. If Mark and Sheila have another child in the future, that child will be born to parents who have grown through their suffering, and have learned how to love one other as equals.

The Stepmother
One performance by the Play Actors club at the New Theatre, London, 13 January 1924

In *The Stepmother,* Githa tackled the question of how women needed to become more financially knowledgeable if they were to achieve both independence and equality with men. Drawing on her experience of males in her own family she aimed to expose to all women, single or married, that to trust a man who presents himself as more financially competent to manage property is a high risk strategy.

After the Married Women's Property Act came into force in 1882, married women had full legal control of all the property they owned at marriage or acquired after it. But this did not stop husbands putting pressure on their wives to sign over control of their property by means of a power of attorney. In writing *The Stepmother,* therefore, Githa was still promoting the importance of women securing their economic independence from men.

As the play begins, young Lois Relph is a naive girl, formerly the companion to a rich old lady, Fanny Gayden, who has left her a fortune – £30,000. Lois falls prey to her benefactor's plausible scoundrel of a widowed brother, Eustace Gayden, who marries her to get his hands on her inheritance. Over the next ten years, Lois, the stepmother of the title, proves a fine mother to Eustace's two young daughters and, although her marriage is not happy, she builds up a successful fashion design business. Unbeknown to Lois, however, her earnings are supporting the family while Eustace is using her inheritance to speculate in high risk business deals. When one of her step-daughters wants to get married Lois promises her a gift of £10,000. This leads to the discovery that Eustace has lost all the money. Lois is only saved from ruin by the actions of Peter, her lover and loyal friend, who forces Eustace to leave the country. Before he departs, Eustace is persuaded to stand aside and not contest his divorce from Lois. Even though clearly disgraced, Eustace presents his enforced departure and divorce as an act of chivalrous martyrdom in which he provides for his wife's future under her lover, Peter's, care.

EUSTACE   Don't you realise I'm taking the whole blame? That I'm making myself the scapegoat for both your sins?
LOIS   I'm very grateful to you, Eustace.
EUSTACE   You do realise?
LOIS   Yes, yes.
EUSTACE   Very well, I'll go further. I'll give you your freedom.
LOIS   My freedom! How can you do that?
EUSTACE   By allowing you to divorce me.

LOIS   Eustace!

EUSTACE Oh you can do it provided I don't defend myself. It's simple
            enough. You write a letter asking me to return. I refuse. God
            knows what the law will make of our married life before it's
            done with it but that is the law. Well?

LOIS   Why are you doing this?

EUSTACE I've told you, for your sake.

LOIS   Do you want your freedom?

EUSTACE I want you to have yours. I don't say that in the years to come
            it mayn't turn out to be the right thing for me too but that
            isn't the point. I want you to see that I'm capable of making
            a sacrifice. I mayn't have been a model husband in some ways
            but I don't want you to think that I haven't thought about your
            future – provided for it, in a sense.

The Stepmother, Act Three[85]

The Stepmother was written almost ten years after the death of Githa's
father. Although there is no suggestion that her father was ever fraudulent
in his financial dealings, the play is suffused with Githa's anger over his
irresponsible handling of money which left her elderly mother reduced to
living in two rooms in Broadstairs. It is not clear who inspired the other
characters in *The Stepmother.* Charlotte Gayden, Eustace's aunt and an earlier
victim of his financial sleight-of-hand, represents a class. Githa describes her
with pitying savagery:

> "Charlotte Gayden is sitting knitting by the fire. She is about sixty
> years of age with a face already old. She carries herself with that gently
> deprecating air which her generation seems to have considered suitable
> to the lady who failed to justify her existence by marriage. All of her life
> has been devoted to filling the gaps left by other people, and the fact that
> she has never had any business of her own in the world has smoothed
> down any individual characteristics she might have had to a dead level of
> adaptability."[86]

This is a biting indictment of a society that cared nothing about its routine
creation of thousands of Charlotte Gaydens. Sadly, *The Stepmother* was only
ever given one performance in 1924 by and to the members of a private club.
Githa's message that women should not sign powers of attorney was not able
to reach very far.

The Policeman's Whistle
First performed at the Croydon Repertory Theatre, Christmas Eve, 1934

When Githa took up her pen again in 1934, after a decade of silence, she began with a children's play and a children's book. Children's literature was, after all, where her career as an author had begun and perhaps she felt the need to build up her confidence by returning to familiar ground. A new edition of *The Glad Book* was published in 1935 by the Artists and Writers Guild, New York. During the same period she wrote *The Policeman's Whistle*, her one full-length play for children.

The Policeman's Whistle demonstrates Githa's understanding of small children. Throughout the play there is plenty of the pantomime-like visual comedy that reduces them to helpless giggles. Written as a Christmas show for the Croydon Repertory Theatre in 1934 it includes a doctor with magic pills that turn people's clothes into the clothes they deserve, and a policeman called Bobby, with a magic whistle that makes people dance whether they want to or not. The story is a classic battle between Good and Evil. The boy King of Airitonia is spoiled and selfish so his people do not mind when his kingdom is taken over by a wicked Emperor, but they change their minds when they find the Emperor is even worse. To the rescue come two children (Jan and Betty), the doctor, and Bobby the policeman. When the wicked Emperor steals the policeman's magic whistle he must be made to give it back before the now reformed King can win back his kingdom. Heroes and heroines retrieve the whistle while the Emperor is sleeping and with various slap-stick touches, the magic whistle forces the Emperor and his evil henchmen to dance themselves into submission.

The King gets his kingdom back and it is time for the children and the doctor to go home. Suddenly a taxi-driver marches down the aisle through the audience and stands by the orchestra rail.

BOBBY	A taxi-driver! What on earth are you doing walking into a theatre like this?
TAXI-DRIVER	I'm interrupting, I am.
BOBBY	You can't interrupt, we're looking for the crown.
BETTY	(*Coming to the footlights with Jan*) What's the matter, taxi driver?
TAXI-DRIVER	Well, miss, it's this way. There's an aeroplane just landed at the theatre door.
JAN AND BETTY	An aeroplane?
TAXI-DRIVER	Yes, and the pilot says he's called for two young ladies

and a Dr Something-or-other to take them home. The
traffic's held up and what he wants to know is when's
this play going to end?

The Policeman's Whistle, **Scene Seven**

The taxi driver is made to wait while the King is crowned and reclaims his
throne to general rejoicing; everyone waves goodbye, and the play ends with a
dash through the audience to catch the aeroplane.

The Policeman's Whistle reads as a delightful play but it has never been
published, nor has it been revived since its debut at Croydon in 1934.

Direct Action
Never performed

Direct Action is a light comedy with a happy ending. Its tone is very different
from Githa's other adult plays; it has none of their brooding power and for
the first time Githa's key theme of economic independence for women is
absent. However, in *Direct Action* Githa challenged herself as well as her
audience. Writing after her daughter, Joan, had made her debut in London
society, it seems Githa finally recognised that she, the playwright who had so
vigorously championed the cause of female emancipation, had overlooked the
call to what *The Vote* in July 1912 had described as "a freer and more vigorous
motherhood"[87]. As a mother she had shackled her daughter with rules similar
to those to which she herself had been subject 50 years earlier. She had failed
to prepare Joan for life in the world of the 1930s and she had damaged their
relationship as a result.

The plot revolves around the conflict between two sisters, Elizabeth and
Stella. Elizabeth is old-fashioned and her children are naive. Her two eldest
nearly get themselves into serious trouble with members of the opposite
sex because they think they know more about life than they really do. Their
peril is compounded by the fact that their mother's restrictive approach has
forced them to deceive her about their friendships and activities, just as Joan
felt forced to deceive Githa. These are children who feel they cannot confide
in their mother or seek advice from her. It is the more liberal Aunt Stella
who comes to the rescue. She uncovers the trouble the young people are
heading for in time to intervene and save the day. And by the end of the play
Elizabeth has no choice but to enter the 20th century.

It is not hard to imagine the conflict between the two sisters in *Direct Action*
as a debate between Githa, the mother of Joan, and Githa as she might

have been had her passionate nature not been crushed by her repressive upbringing.

ELIZABETH *I've tried to keep my boy straight and good – I've made a home where my children could grow up happy and innocent, as we did.*

STELLA *Oh for God's sake don't dramatise. And I didn't grow up happy and innocent. I was restless and ignorant.*

ELIZABETH *Whose fault was that?*

STELLA *Our parents were old enough to be two generations behind us and that's what's wrong with you, only you don't know it.*

ELIZABETH *Wrong with <u>me</u>?*

STELLA *How much have you told your children about themselves?*

ELIZABETH *I don't know what you're talking about.*

STELLA *Elizabeth, you've been married and had children – even you must have gleaned a faint idea of what human feeling can be.*

ELIZABETH *In its proper place.*

STELLA *It isn't in its proper place in the world today.*

ELIZABETH *I don't know anything about the world today and I don't want to.*

STELLA *It's your business to know. It isn't fair to bring up children out of their generation – it's cruel and dangerous.*

Direct Action, Act Three[88]

Direct Action has some delightful moments of comedy – for example, a quarrel and then an actual fight between Elizabeth and Stella. This episode is so reminiscent of their behaviour as children that their old nanny, who still lives with the Ellison family, finds herself saying she will have to "tell their father" of their behaviour. However, whether *Direct Action* could ever be performed is an open question. The story focuses on a child rearing regime that was already seriously out-of-date by the time Githa wrote the play. Audiences could have struggled to see the relevance of the story even in 1937/38 when it was written. A 21st century audience would be baffled that Elizabeth Ellison could ever have thought it appropriate to protect her children so completely and so nearly disastrously from the realities of life. As a comedy it could provoke laughter, but probably nowadays not always in the places Githa intended. Maybe in 20 or 30 years' time *Direct Action* will have become enough of a period piece for a modern audience to accept it more readily. If not, *Direct Action* may be destined never to be performed.

EPILOGUE

Finding Githa

"The truth is that the English people have in Miss Sowerby a positive genius, who has begun early but not abnormally, and who gives abundant evidence that she is destined to take rank with the world's best latter-day writers and thinkers."[89]

Journalist Phil Farnum put it more succinctly and clearly than most in his 1912 review, but he was not alone in his appraisal of the importance of Githa's work in *Rutherford & Son*. There is no doubt that Githa Sowerby was briefly recognised for the skilled dramatist that she was, but we cannot avoid the fact that the British theatre, having found Githa Sowerby in 1912, promptly put her down somewhere and forgot both her and the messages she was trying to convey through her plays.

As a playwright Githa Sowerby demonstrates great insight into character and motivation. Her dialogue is powerful and reminiscent of real speech; her characters appear as living beings. Her style has been compared at various times to Ibsen, Gorky, Galsworthy and Pinero. So why were Githa Sowerby's plays virtually ignored by the British theatre after that first success of *Rutherford & Son*?

Undoubtedly, sexism in the theatre and sexism in society had a significant part to play but other factors contributed. Githa was very reserved; she hated the trappings of fame. She disliked speaking in public, and did not want to become a public figure. She gave journalists as little information as possible about herself and she did not build on the press contacts she had made once the sensation over the success of *Rutherford & Son* had died down. She was not part of any feminist groups so there was no ready-made network of female supporters to give her confidence and keep alive the memory of her work.

Timing was also an issue. Just as the timing of her first play had been most fortunate historically and politically, the timing of her other plays was not. Githa was slow to produce the scripts of new plays. This allowed her to drop more readily out of the minds of the public and out of the minds of the movers and shakers of British theatre. By the time Githa had finished the script of *A Man and Some Women*, suffragist Lena Ashwell had leased the Kingsway Theatre to Granville Barker and, once he rejected the script and other theatres followed suit, the First World War finally destroyed any

chance of *A Man and Some Women* getting a run in London. Sir George
Alexander, last of the actor-managers, accepted *Sheila* in 1917, but he died
two years later. As British theatre was still unsubsidised, the dawn of the era
of commercial syndicates rendered a serious play like *The Stepmother* too risky
a venture. Githa was not interested in writing the drawing-room comedies
that became the fodder of the commercial theatre managements. And it did
not help that, in her disappointment over the failure of *The Stepmother* to get
a London run in 1924, Githa suspended her writing career as a dramatist for
almost ten years.

Nearly a century has passed since *Rutherford & Son* first appeared in 1912.
It was revived in 1980 in a shortened form edited by Micheline Wandor and
directed by Julie Holledge for feminist theatre group Mrs Worthington's
Daughters. After that, a steady trickle of productions of *Rutherford & Son*
appeared at a range of theatres – Wyn Jones directed the play at the New
End Theatre, Hampstead, in 1988 and Malcolm Hebden at the Stephen
Joseph Theatre, Scarborough, in 1991. Michael Fox produced one version for
BBC Radio 4's *Monday Play* in 1992; Katie Mitchell produced another at
the National Theatre in 1994. *Rutherford & Son* was performed at Salisbury
Playhouse under the direction of Joanna Read in 2001 and at Manchester
Royal Exchange Theatre by Sarah Frankcom in 2005. There was another
production by Richard Corley for the Mint Theatre Company of New York
in 2001, and the Shaw Festival at Niagara-on-the-Lake, Ontario, Canada,
enjoyed a success with director Jackie Maxwell's version in 2004. Jackie
Maxwell then went on to produce an acclaimed version of *The Stepmother* in
2008. Since 1996 there have also been a number of amateur productions of
Rutherford & Son.

So *Rutherford & Son* has belatedly been given some recognition nationally
and internationally as the ground-breaking feminist play that it is. But at the
time of writing this book in early 2009, most of the people of Tyneside still
do not know that Githa Sowerby was a member of the Sowerby glassmaking
dynasty, that she lived in Gateshead for the first 18 years of her life, or that
she wrote a play whose story reflects that industrial heritage.

However this is soon to be put right for, in September 2009, *Rutherford
& Son* will come home. Githa Sowerby's play will enjoy its first ever
production on Tyneside at Northern Stage in Newcastle in a co-production
with Threshold Theatre, directed by Richard Beecham. If she was alive
today, Githa would be astonished and very happy that her plays are being
remembered. But full justice has not yet been done to her achievements while
the rest of Githa's plays are left unpublished and remain still largely unknown
in this country.

Progress always carries a risk. To crusade for change is dangerous for, to borrow the words of John Kaye Kendall's favourite author, Lewis Carroll:

> ... *beware of the day*
> *If your Snark be a Boojum, for then*
> *You will softly and suddenly vanish away,*
> *And never be met with again!* [90]

Having found Githa Sowerby once more it is up to us to see that British theatre gives her the respect due to her, so that she does not vanish a second time.

Sowerby family tree

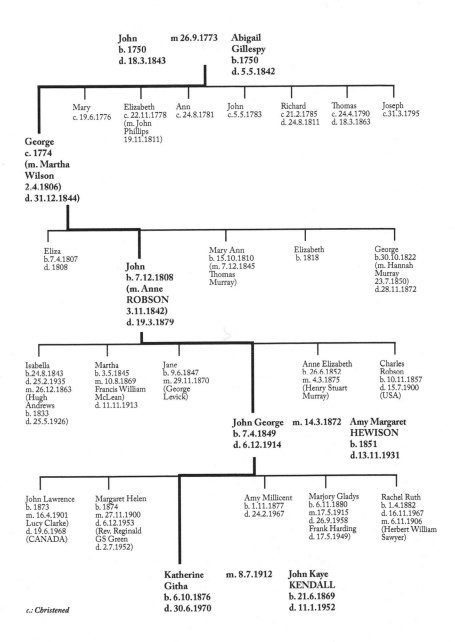

John
b. 1750
d. 18.3.1843

m 26.9.1773

Abigail
Gillespy
b.1750
d. 5.5.1842

Mary
c. 19.6.1776

Elizabeth
c. 22.11.1778
(m. John
Phillips
19.11.1811)

Ann
c. 24.8.1781

John
c.5.5.1783

Richard
c 21.2.1785
d. 24.8.1811

Thomas
c. 24.4.1790
d. 18.3.1863

Joseph
c.31.3.1795

George
c. 1774
(m. Martha
Wilson
2.4.1806)
d. 31.12.1844)

Eliza
b.7.4.1807
d. 1808

John
b. 7.12.1808
(m. Anne
ROBSON
3.11.1842)
d. 19.3.1879

Mary Ann
b. 15.10.1810
(m. 7.12.1845
Thomas
Murray)

Elizabeth
b. 1818

George
b.30.10.1822
(m. Hannah
Murray
23.7.1850)
d.28.11.1872

Isabella
b.24.8.1843
d. 25.2.1935
m. 26.12.1863
(Hugh
Andrews
b. 1833
d. 25.5.1926)

Martha
b. 3.5.1845
m. 10.8.1869
Francis William
McLean)
d. 11.11.1913

Jane
b. 9.6.1847
m. 29.11.1870
(George
Levick)

Anne Elizabeth
b. 26.6.1852
m. 4.3.1875
(Henry Stuart
Murray)

Charles
Robson
b. 10.11.1857
d. 15.7.1900
(USA)

John George
b. 7.4.1849
d. 6.12.1914

m. 14.3.1872

Amy Margaret
HEWISON
b. 1851
d.13.11.1931

John Lawrence
b. 1873
m. 16.4.1901
Lucy Clarke)
d. 19.6.1968
(CANADA)

Margaret Helen
b. 1874
m. 27.11.1900
d. 6.12.1953
(Rev. Reginald
GS Green
d. 2.7.1952)

Amy Millicent
b. 1.11.1877
d. 24.2.1967

Marjory Gladys
b. 6.11.1880
m.17.5.1915
d. 26.9.1958
Frank Harding
d. 17.5.1949)

Rachel Ruth
b. 1.4.1882
d. 16.11.1967
m. 6.11.1906
(Herbert William
Sawyer)

Katherine
Githa
b. 6.10.1876
d. 30.6.1970

m. 8.7.1912

John Kaye
KENDALL
b. 21.6.1869
d. 11.1.1952

c.: Christened

131

Books, plays and song lyrics by Githa Sowerby

1906 *The Wise Book* (JM Dent, now Orion Books)
1907 *Childhood* (Chatto & Windus)
 The Bumbletoes (Chatto & Windus)
1908 *Yesterday's Children* (Chatto & Windus)
 Love Me (English lyrics for song by Tosti)
1909 *Grimms' Fairy Tales* (Grant Richards)
 The Happy Book (Henry Frowde/Hodder & Stoughton)
 Once More (English lyrics for song by Tosti)
1910 *Little Plays for Little People* (plays for children) (Hodder & Stoughton)
 Little Stories for Little People (from The Arabian Nights) (Hodder & Stoughton)
 Little Songs for Little People (song book) (Henry Frowde/Hodder & Stoughton)
 Who? (English lyrics for song by Tosti)
 Two Little Songs: Could I But Tell and *I Cannot Tell* (English lyrics for songs by Tosti)
1911 *The Merry Book* (Humphrey Milford/Oxford University Press)
 My Birthday (Humphrey Milford/Oxford University Press)
 Now (English lyrics for song by Tosti)
1912 *Rutherford & Son* (full-length play) (Sidgwick & Jackson)
 Poems of Childhood (Humphrey Milford/Oxford University Press)
 Little Plays for School and Home (Hodder & Stoughton)
 Before Breakfast (one-act play) unpublished/Samuel French*
 First Waltz (English lyrics for song by Tosti)
1913 *A Man and Some Women* (full-length play) – unpublished/Samuel French*
1915 *Cinderella* (Henry Frowde/Hodder & Stoughton)
 The Gay Book (Henry Frowde/Hodder & Stoughton)
 The Pretty Book (Henry Frowde/Hodder & Stoughton)
 The Dainty Book (Humphrey Milford/Oxford University Press)
1916 *The Bright Book* (Henry Frowde/Hodder & Stoughton)
1917 *Sheila* (full-length play) – unpublished/Samuel French*
1918 *The Bonnie Book* (Humphrey Milford/Oxford University Press)
1919 *Childhood* (Chatto & Windus)
1920 *The Dainty Book* (Humphrey Milford/Oxford University Press)
1921 *The Wise Book* (JM Dent – now Orion Books)
1923 *The Stepmother* (full-length play) – unpublished in Githa's lifetime* but
published in 2008 by the Shaw Festival Theatre, Ontario, Canada
1925 *Poems of Childhood* (Humphrey Milford/Oxford University Press)
1934 *The Policeman's Whistle* (children's play) – unpublished/Samuel French*
1935 *The Glad Book* (Artists and Writers Guild, New York)
1937/38 *Direct Action* (full-length play) – unpublished/Samuel French*

* Samuel French & Co administers the literary estate (including unpublished plays) for all Githa's plays on behalf of her daughter.

A note of books & paintings by John George Sowerby

Illustrated books

1880	*Come With Me* (R Robinson & Co, Newcastle-upon-Tyne)
	Afternoon Tea (Frederick Warne & Co)
1881	*At Home* (Marcus Ward & Co)
1882	*At Home Again* (Marcus Ward & Co)
1888	*Jimmy: Scenes from the Life of a Black Doll* (G Routledge & Sons)
1889	*Young Maids and Old China* (G Routledge & Sons)
1895	*Rooks and Their Neighbours* (Gay & Bird) – text also written by JGS

Paintings

(a) Painted while living at Ravenshill
1879   *Twilight*
1880   *Partenhall*
1883   *Poppies*
1884   *Strayed*
1885   *Plum Blossoms*

(b) Painted at Wall-on-Tyne, Northumberland
1894   *A Quiet Wood*
        A Sexton's House

(c) Painted at Chollerton, Northumberland
1897   *The Erring Burn*
        A Garden
        A Flowering Fruit Tree trained on an Espalier
1898   *The Month of Leaves*

(d) Painted at Boxted House near Colchester
1899   *The Rattle Beck*
1901   *The Flooded Meadow*
        The Amber Vale

(e) Painted at Sutton Courtenay, Berks
1904   *The Avon*
1909   *Michaelmas Daisies*

f) Painted at Wye Gate, Monmouthshire
The Daffodil Wood (past Symonds Yat Station)

Works whose dates are not yet identified
A Landscape in Spring with a Nun Walking Among Daffodils, A Rocky Stream Overhung with Trees, The Summons, A Milkmaid, Meadowsweet in an Orchard, A Thatched Cottage with Arum Lilies and Roses, Cottage with Garden, Geese in Summer Meadow, Walking Among the Daffodils near a Stream, Hunting Quail, Hollyhocks in Bloom, Flower Garden, A Field of Thistles, A Rocky Stream, Pigeon Shooting, A Meadow in Winter, Spring, Summer, Autumn, Winter, Stonehenge

Acknowledgements

This book could not have been written without the help of a great number of people and I gratefully acknowledge their contribution.

First on that list must be Githa's daughter Joan Smith, without whose immense contribution to this book I could never have tackled the task of 'Looking for Githa'; I have written about this extensively in the preface. Second on my list for thanks must be indefatigable family history researcher Tom Cruikshanks. Tom's wife Frances is related to the Sowerby family through marriage, and for several years Tom has been researching the life and achievements of the Murray, Bailey and Sowerby families of Tyneside. I was put in touch with Tom on 14 April 2008 by Simon Cottle, the UK's foremost authority on Sowerby glass, and Tom and I agreed to share all our research findings from then on. Genealogical research is like unravelling a detective story and is normally a solitary activity, so working with another family history researcher was a new and hugely enjoyable experience for both of us. Tackling the various written sources of information between us doubled the ground we could cover while halving the length of time the research would take. Soon we were in daily email and phone contact, and this continued until mid-2009 when the pre-publication draft of *Looking for Githa* was complete.

I would never have met Joan or Tom without the two intermediaries previously mentioned; so special thanks are due to Paul Taylor of Samuel French & Co and Simon Cottle of Bonham Fine Art Auctioneers and Valuers. In addition I must thank Simon Cottle for permission to quote freely from *Sowerby: Gateshead Glass*, his fascinating account of the 19th century history of the New Stourbridge Glass Works and the Sowerby's Ellison Glass Works in Gateshead. This book is the standard work on Sowerby glass, and Simon's permission to draw freely it saved hours of additional research.

Special thanks are also due to Joan and Shannon Jolley of Port Moody, British Columbia, grand-daughter and great-grand-daughter of Githa Sowerby's elder brother Lawrence who emigrated to Canada in 1912. Shannon and Joan Jolley spent hours in early 2009 sorting, photographing and re-touching more than 200 historic Sowerby photographs and documents and emailing them to England. Most of the family photographs that appear in this book are here only because of their work. I must also include here grateful thanks to Leila Muldrew of the Victoria Genealogical Society, Canada, and Catherine George of the Peninsula News, Vancouver Island, Canada, without whose dogged determination and skill we would never have traced Shannon and Joan Jolley and the other descendants of Lawrence Sowerby in Canada. Without the piece of the puzzle they provided, these two groups of Sowerby descendants might never have re-established contact.

Thank you to the ever patient John Hall of the Local Studies Library in Gateshead, who gave invaluable help in tracing Sowerby property records and newspaper cuttings about the Sowerby family in general and Githa Sowerby in particular. Helen Smailes, Senior Curator at the National Gallery of Scotland, provided detailed information about the history of James Guthrie's portrait of Margaret Helen Sowerby. Sotheby's, Christie's and Bonham's provided lists of the paintings by John George Sowerby offered for sale on the open market in recent years. Ray and Dorothy Williams supplied the introduction to Damien Hirst and Minky Sloane, providing photographs of the main staircase and the 'heaven and hell window' at Toddington Manor. Thanks are due to the Surrey History Centre and the Coroner for Surrey for permission to use information obtained from the record of the inquest that examined the circumstances of the 1952 accidental death of Githa Sowerby's husband, John Kaye Kendall. Elmare Broodryk provided the contact with Zahida Sirkhotte of the National Library of South Africa, who facilitated access to Githa's brother Lawrence's account of his year with the British South African Police, while the British South African Police Association provided further information about Lawrence Sowerby's service in South Africa.

Julie Holledge, Professor of Drama at Adelaide University, Australia, supplied information and memorabilia from the adaptation of *Rutherford & Son* staged in London in 1980 by feminist theatre group Mrs Worthington's Daughters. Joanna Falck, Literary Manager at the Shaw Festival Theatre in Niagara-on-the-Lake, Ontario, Canada, contributed information about the Shaw Festival's productions of Githa Sowerby's plays *Rutherford & Son* in 2004 and *The Stepmother* in 2008.

Thanks are due to Ian Whitehead of Tyne & Wear Museums Service for information about the history of rowing on Tyneside; to the Garrick Club for information about their members in the early 20th century and a tour of the club; to Kensington Local Studies Library for information about the Kensington War Supplies Depot; to the British Schools Expeditionary Society and to Katherine Lambert for information about Murray Levick; to Winchester College for information about Lawrence Sowerby's time at the college; to Sue Donnelly, archivist to the Fabian Society at the London School of Economics, for the provision of information, and to the Fabian Society for permission to use it; to Dorothy Hall of Chester-le-Street Heritage Society for information and a photograph of Whitehill, George Sowerby Snr's final home; the staff of the Department of Vital Statistics, Government of British Columbia, Canada, for the provision of the probate files for Lawrence and Lucy Sowerby and to the Wasa and District Historical Association, British Columbia, for information about Lawrence and Lucy Sowerby from the book *Kootenay Ripples*. I also gratefully acknowledge the help of the Foreign and Colonial section of the British Library, of the BBC Sound Archives at the British Library; of the Registries of Births, Deaths and Marriages in various parts of the country and of the various Probate Offices, whose staff have all been extremely helpful but who are too numerous to mention individually. In addition, the enthusiastic encouragement of Jayne Richards, David Mathews and Michael Walling of Rose Bruford College, Sidcup, was very much appreciated as research into Githa Sowerby's background, life and achievements progressed.

That the launch of this book is to become part of a Githa Sowerby Festival on Tyneside in September 2009 is due to the enthusiasm, hard work and commitment of Richard Beecham of Threshold Theatre, Erica Whyman of Northern Stage, Members and Officers of Gateshead and Newcastle Councils, Claire Malcolm of New Writing North, and to Rebecca Jenkins, publisher's editor for *Looking for Githa*. Grateful thanks are due to the Northern Rock Foundation and Arts Council England, without whose support this publication would not have been possible. To see Githa Sowerby at last given the recognition she deserves, and to be part of that process, is wonderful.

Finally, my heartfelt thanks to Frances Cruikshanks and Bernard Riley for their patience while Tom Cruikshanks and I spent hours in email and phone contact with one another, separately visited libraries and archives, pored over documents, conducted interviews by telephone and in person, and wrote, corrected, added to, and refined the text of *Looking for Githa*. If any errors remain in the text, the responsibility is mine.

Pat Riley
Leeds, June 2009

Bibliography

Lena Ashwell, *Myself a Player,* Michael Joseph (1936)

Gayle Austin, *Feminist Theories for Dramatic Criticism,* University of Michigan Press (1990)

Lilian Baylis and Cicely Hamilton, *The Old Vic,* Jonathan Cape (1926)

Charles Brookfield, *Random Reminiscences,* Edward Arnold (1902)

Charles and Frances Brookfield, *Mrs Brookfield and Her Circle*, Pitman & Sons (1908)

Douglas Carter, *Boxted,* CJW Publishing (2006)

Dawn and Peter Cope, *Illustrators of Postcards from the Nursery,* East-West Publications (1978)

Dawn and Peter Cope, *Postcards from the Nursery,* Clarendon (2000)

Simon Cottle, *Sowerby: Gateshead Glass,* Tyne & Wear Museum Service (1986)

Linda Fitzsimmons & Viv Gardner, *New Woman Plays,* Methuen (1991)

Deborah Gorham, *The Victorian Girl and the Feminine Ideal,* Indiana University Press (1982)

Cicely Hamilton, *Marriage as a Trade,* Dodo Press (2008)/Chapman & Hall (1909)

Cicely Hamilton, *The Truth About Man,* Hutchinson & Co (1905)

Peter Hunt, *Introducing Children's Literature,* OUP (1994)

Laurence Ince, *The South Wales Iron Industry 1750-1885,* Ferric (1993)

John Kendall, *Rhymes of the East and Re-Collected Verses,* Archibald Constable (1905)

John Kendall, *Dum-Dum, His Selected Verses,* Harrap (1947)

Katherine Lambert, *The Longest Winter,* Pimlico (2002)

G Murray Levick, *Antarctic Penguins,* Heineman (1914)

James MacFarlane (ed), *Cambridge Companion to Ibsen,* Cambridge University Press (1994)

Sheilagh Murray, *The Peacock and the Lions,* Oriel (1982)

Edward R Pease, *The History of the Fabian Society,* Echo Library (1916)

CB Purdom, *Granville Barker,* Harvard (1956)

George Rowell (ed), *Victorian Dramatic Criticism,* Methuen (1971)

Joanna Russ, *How to Suppress Women's Writing,* Women's Press (1984)

Francesco Sanvitale, *The Song of a Life,* Ashgate (2004)

George Bernard Shaw, *The Intelligent Woman's Guide to Socialism and Capitalism,* Constable (1929)

George Bernard Shaw, *The Quintessence of Ibsenism,* Brentano (1904)

Githa Sowerby, *The Wise Book,* JM Dent (1906)

   Childhood, Chatto & Windus (1907)

   The Bumbletoes, Chatto & Windus (1907)

   Yesterday's Children, Chatto & Windus (1907)

   Grimms' Fairy Tales, Grant Richards (1909)

   The Happy Book, Henry Frowde (1909)

   Little Plays for Little People, Hodder & Stoughton (1910)

   Little Songs for Little People, Henry Frowde (1910)

Little Stories for Little People, Hodder & Stoughton (1910)

The Merry Book, Humphrey Milford (1911)

My Birthday, Humphrey Milford (1911)

Poems of Childhood, Humphrey Milford (1912)

Rutherford & Son, Sidgwick & Jackson (1912)

Before Breakfast (1912) unpublished/Samuel French

Little Plays for School and Home (1912)

A Man and Some Women (1913) unpublished/Samuel French

Cinderella, Henry Frowde (1915)

The Gay Book, Henry Frowde (1915)

The Pretty Book, Henry Frowde (1915)

The Dainty Book, Humphrey Milford (1915)

The Bright Book, Henry Frowde (1916)

Sheila (1917) unpublished/Samuel French

The Bonnie Book, Humphrey Milford (1918)

Childhood, Chatto & Windus (1919)

The Dainty Book, Humphrey Milford (1920)

The Wise Book, JM Dent (1921)

The Stepmother (1924) unpublished/Samuel French in UK but published in Canada by Shaw Festival Theatre (2008)

Poems of Childhood, Humphrey Milford (1925)

The Policeman's Whistle (1934) unpublished/Samuel French

The Glad Book, Artists and Writers Guild, New York (1935)

Direct Action (1937/38) unpublished/Samuel French

John George Sowerby, *Come With Me,* Robinson & Co (1880)

Afternoon Tea, Warne & Co (1880)

At Home, Marcus Ward & Co (1881)

At Home Again, Marcus Ward & Co (1886)

Jimmy, Scenes from the Life of a Black Doll, Told By Himself, Routledge & Co (1888)

Young Maids and Old China, Routledge & Co (1889)

Rooks and Their Neighbours, Gay & Bird (1895)

Ray Strachey, *The Cause,* Virago (1978)

John Stuart Mill, *On the Subjection of Women,* Penguin (2006)

Ian Whitehead, *The Sporting Tyne,* Gateshead Council (2002)

Lis Whitelaw, *The Life and Rebellious Times of Cicely Hamilton,* The Women's Press (1990)

Mary Wollstonecraft, *Vindication of the Rights of Women:* Penguin (1975)

Wasa Historical Society, *Kootenay Ripples,* Wasa Historical Society, Box 172 Wasa, BC, Canada VOB 2K0 (2002)

Endnotes

1 *Rutherford & Son:* Sowerby, Githa – Sidgwick & Jackson (1912), p22
2 See, for example, *How to Suppress Women's Writing:* Russ, Joanna – The Women's Press (1983)
3 Reviews taken from the jacket of *Rutherford & Son:* Sowerby, Githa – Sidgwick & Jackson (1912)
4 *Rutherford & Son:* Sowerby, Githa – Sidgwick & Jackson (1912)
5 *'Remarkable Play by a Young English Miss':* Howard, Keble: *Daily Mail,* 9 February 1912
6 Undated and unreferenced magazine cutting obtained from Local Studies Library, Gateshead
7 *Sowerby: Gateshead Glass:* Cottle, Simon – Tyne & Wear Museum Service (1986), p9
8 Ibid: p12
9 Ibid
10 Ibid, p17
11 Ibid, p17
12 Ibid, p21
13 *The Peacock and the Lion:* Murray, Sheilagh – Oriel Press (1982), pp9-10
14 Githa's brother Lawrence stated in an undated letter to his son Eric that Daniel Robson was then the head of the Robson clan – one of the ancient English Border country clans whose numbers also included the Percy, Elliot and Armstrong clans. Letter made available by kind permission of Shannon and Joan Jolley, Port Moody, British Columbia
15 *Sowerby: Gateshead Glass:* Cottle, Simon – Tyne & Wear Museum Service (1986), p22
16 *The South Wales Iron Industry 1780-1885*: Ince, L – Longmans (1993)
17 *The Times,* 1 June 1956
18 The 1871 census shows Charles Robson Sowerby aged 15 as a pupil of Prestonville School, a school for the sons of gentlemen, in Hove, Sussex
19 US Federal Census 1900
20 The Foothills Genealogical Society's Index to Jefferson County Colorado Marriages 1860-1899 shows that this marriage took place on 3 May 1898
21 *The Peacock and the Lions:* Murray, Sheilagh – Oriel Press (1982), p13
22 For more information about the history of rowing on Tyneside, see *The Sporting Tyne:* Whitehead, Ian – Gateshead Council (2002)
23 *Sowerby: Gateshead Glass:* Cottle, Simon – Tyne & Wear Museum Service (1986), p25
24 *Maud, A Monodrama,* Part II – Alfred Lord Tennyson
25 For example, John Sowerby locked the men out in 1872 when they formed a new trade society to represent the interests of pressed glass workers. Prior to this, the pressed glass workers had been unorganised, unlike the glass blowers with whom John Sowerby had previously crossed swords
26 UK census 1891

27 There is no property named Chollerton House on the 1867 or 1897 maps of the Chollerton area
28 *Sowerby: Gateshead Glass:* Cottle, Simon – Tyne & Wear Museum Service (1986), pp26-31
29 *The Basis* is reproduced here by kind permission of the Fabian Society
30 Reproduced here by kind permission of the Fabian Society
31 *The History of the Fabian Society:* Pease, Edward R – Echo (2006), pp103-104
32 Ibid
33 *My Birthday:* pictured by Millicent Sowerby, told by Githa Sowerby, Henry Frowde & Hodder & Stoughton (1911)
34 Chatto & Windus
35 Henry Frowde (Hodder & Stoughton)
36 Both published by Humphrey Milford (Oxford University Press)
37 On his return to England from Canada in 1860, the Reverend Kendall was first Curate of St John's and then Vicar of St Mark's in Notting Hill. After this he served as Vicar of Perry Hill and ended his career as a Curate in Southsea and Alverstoke
38 As John Kaye Kendall's service records have not been released to the National Archives by the Ministry of Defence, it has not been possible to confirm whether he had any other health problems as a result of his service in India in addition to incipient deafness
39 *Rhymes of the East and Re-Collected Verses:* Kendall, J – Archibald Constable & Co Ltd (1905)
40 *New Woman Plays:* edited by Fitzsimmons, L and Gardner, V – Methuen (1991), p29
41 Sos Eltis: *"The Fallen Woman in Edwardian Drama": Suffrage, Sex and the Single Girl": http:/muse.jhu.edu/demo/english_literature_in_transition/vo/50/1eltis.html,* accessed 10.3.2008
42 *Rutherford & Son:* Sowerby, Githa – Sidgwick & Jackson (1912) – Act One, p9
43 *'Rutherford & Son – a Great Suffrage Play': The Vote,* 20 July 1912
44 *'When Lovely English Miss Turns to Playwriting':* New York Times: 9 December 1912
45 Humphrey Milford (Oxford University Press)
46 Hodder & Stoughton
47 *Chains:* Baker, E, in *New Woman Plays:* Gardner, V, Fitzsimmons, L – Methuen (1991)
48 For the full story of the experiences of the Northern Party on the Scott expedition, read *The Longest Winter:* Lambert, Katherine – Smithsonian Books (2004)
49 Appendix 3 lists some of John George Sowerby's paintings
50 *Maud, a Monodrama,* Part II: Alfred Lord Tennyson
51 *'In Kensington Square': Punch* magazine, 30 May and 27 June 1917
52 Undated article in *Ladies' Pictorial*
53 *World:* 12.6.1917, quoted in *New Woman Plays:* Gardner, V, and Fitzsimmons, L (eds) – Methuen (1991), p136
54 Reported in the *Cumberland News,* 16 February 1918
55 *The Cause:* Strachey, Ray – Virago, London (1978)

56 Ibid, p348

57 The only surviving letter from Curtis Brown concerning *The Stepmother* is about the possible sale of the Scandinavian rights in December 1923 for a fee of £40. It is not known, however, if any performances of *The Stepmother* then took place in any of the Scandinavian countries

58 Theatre programme for *The Stepmother*: New Theatre, 13 January 1924

59 *Illustrated Sporting and Dramatic:* 26 January 1924

60 *Daily Chronicle,* 14 January 1924

61 The date on which Githa left the Fabian Society is not known

62 Information from the inquest record is included by kind permission of the Surrey History Centre

63 Ibid

64 This is the only known personal letter of Githa's still in existence, and is reproduced here by kind permission of Shannon and Joan Jolley, Port Moody, British Columbia

65 Poem by Githa Sowerby in undated and unreferenced newspaper cutting re *Rutherford & Son* -1912

66 Ibid

67 Samuel French & Co administers the literary estate for all Githa's plays on behalf of her daughter

68 *The Old Vic:* Hamilton, Cicely, and Baylis, Lillian – Butler and Tanner Ltd (1926), p161

69 *The Quintessence of Ibsenism:* Shaw, George Bernard – Brentano (1904), was first presented as a lecture to the Fabians and subsequently expanded into a book

70 *Ibsen and the Realistic Problem Drama:* Hemmer, Bjorn, in *The Cambridge Guide to Ibsen* – Cambridge University Press (1994), p70

71 *Little Plays for Little People:* Sowerby, Githa – Hodder & Stoughton (1910)

72 *Rutherford & Son:* Sowerby, Githa – Methuen (1994), p64

73 Ibid, p65

74 Ibid, p1

75 *Before Breakfast:* Sowerby, Githa – Samuel French & Co (1913), p9

76 Ibid, p18

77 *A Man and Some Women:* Sowerby, Githa – unpublished text – Samuel French & Co

78 Ibid

79 *A Doll's House:* Henrik Ibsen

80 *Marriage as a Trade*: Hamilton, Cicely – Dodo Press, 16 May 2008, p81

81 *Sheila:* Sowerby, Githa – Act One, p1 (unpublished manuscript – Samuel French & Co)

82 Ibid

83 Ibid

84 *World: 12.6.1917*, quoted in *New Woman Plays:* Gardner, V, and Fitzsimmons, L (eds): Methuen (1991), p136

85 *The Stepmother:* Sowerby, Githa: The Academy of the Shaw Festival and the Women's Press, Canada (2008), pp131-132

86 Ibid, p11

87 *'Rutherford & Son – a Great Suffrage Play': The Vote*, 20 July 1912

88 *Direct Action:* Sowerby, Githa – unpublished manuscript – Samuel French & Co, Act Three, p19

89 Undated and unreferenced magazine cutting obtained from Local Studies Library, Gateshead

90 *Fit the Third, The Baker's Tale, The Hunting of the Snark:* Carroll, Lewis